GW00383508

FRIENDS
&
FRIENDSHIP

Vol. 1 – USA & CANADA

THE POET
Summer 2021

Compiled by Robin Barratt

THE POET

A leading international online poetry magazine, recognized for both its quarterly themed collections, and its interviews with poets worldwide; looking at their work and their words, and what motivates and inspires them to write.

Interviews, profiles, articles, quarterly collections, Poet of the Week, Poetry Courses and Young Poets.

www.ThePoetMagazine.org

~

FRIENDS & FRIENDSHIP
Vol.1 – USA & CANADA

Published by THE POET

ISBN: 9798538022373

© THE POET, July2021, and all the authors herein

All rights reserved. No part of this publication may be reproduced, distributed, or transmitted in any form or by any means, including photocopying, recording, or other electronic or mechanical methods, without the prior written permission of the publisher, except in the case of brief quotations embodied in critical reviews and certain other non-commercial uses permitted by copyright law. For permission requests, email the publisher at the address below.

E: Robin@ThePoetMagazine.org

Cover image and design: Canva
www.Canva.com

Compiled and published for THE POET by:
Robin Barratt Publishing
Affordable Publishing Services

www.RobinBarratt.co.uk

THE POET is sponsored by:

Poems Over Coffee

John Johnson

www.PoemsOverCoffee.com

"John Johnson is a proud sponsor of THE POET."

If you would also like to sponsor THE POET, please go to:

www.thepoetmagazine.org/support-us

THANK YOU!

THANK YOU TO EVERYONE, EVERYWHERE SUPPORTING THE POET; WITHOUT YOUR HELP WE WOULDN'T BE ABLE TO CONTINUE SHOWCASING INSPIRING POETS AND PUBLISHING AMAZING POETRY ...

... AND WHAT A DULL WORLD THAT WOULD BE!

Love poetry?

Please support or sponsor us too; we are a not-for-profit, so everything goes back into showcasing poets and promoting poetry from around the world.

Go to the website for further details:

www.ThePoetMagazine.org

OTHER COLLECTIONS FROM THE POET

FAITH
With 234 contributions from 151 poets in 36 countries, and from 30 states in the US; published in two volumes, FAITH is probably one of the largest and most significant international collections of poetry on the theme of faith ever published.
Vol. 1 - USA – ISBN: 9798740844695
Vol. 2 - REST OF THE WORLD – ISBN: 9798740924557

CHILDHOOD
With over 300 contributions from 152 poets in 33 countries worldwide, and across 28 States in the USA, CHILDHOOD is in two volumes and is our most popular collection to date.
Vol. 1 - USA - ISBN: 9798564862332
Vol. 2 – REST OF THE WORLD - ISBN: 9798593564696

CHRISTMAS
With over 150 contributions from 97 poets in 34 countries, CHRISTMAS is probably one of the largest international anthologies of Christmas poetry ever published.
153 poems / 275 pages.
ISBN: 9798564859837

A NEW WORLD - Rethinking our lives post-pandemic.
Sixty-seven poets from around the world all writing on the theme of A NEW WORLD; exploring life post-pandemic.
115 poems/225 pages
ISBN: 9798696477084

SUMMER 2020 – ON THE ROAD Volumes 1 & 2
With one hundred and twenty poets from around the world, ON THE ROAD, is probably one of the largest international anthologies of travel poetry ever published.
Vol.1: 135 poems / 240 pages
ISBN: 9798640673593
Vol. 2: 117 poems / 245 pages
ISBN: 9798665956312

SPRING 2020 – WAR & BATTLE
Fifty-four poets from around the world all writing on the theme of WAR & BATTLE.
103 poems/215 pages.
ISBN: 9798629604594

WINTER 2019 - THE SEASONS
Thirty-four poets from around the world all writing on the theme of
THE SEASONS.
80 poems/129 pages.
ISBN: 9798600084445

AUTUMN 2019 - LOVE
THE POET's very first collection. Twenty-nine poets from around the
world all writing on the theme of LOVE.
73 poems/119 pages.
ISBN: 9781699169612

CONTENTS

143. Joan Leotta - CALABASH, NORTH CAROLINA
147. John Laue - LA SELVA BEACH, CALIFORNIA
149. Janet McCann - COLLEGE STATION, TEXAS
153. Jill Sharon Kimmelman - DELAWARE
157. Debi Schmitz Noriega - DES MOINES, IOWA
159. Susan Zeni - MINNEAPOLIS, MINNESOTA
161. Ed Ahern - FAIRFIELD, CONNECTICUT
163. Alonzo "zO" Gross - BETHLEHEM, PENNSYLVANIA
165. Lisa Molina - AUSTIN, TEXAS
169. Bernadette Perez - BELEN, NEW MEXICO
173. Wilda Morris - BOLINGBROOK, ILLINOIS
175. William R. Stoddart - PITTSBURGH, PENNSYLVANIA
177. R. Bremner - GLEN RIDGE, NEW JERSEY
179. Rose Menyon Heflin - MADISON, WISCONSIN
183. Nancy Shiffrin - SANTA MONICA, CALIFORNIA
185. Rita B. Rose - LONG ISLAND, NEW YORK
187. Mariana Mcdonald - ATLANTA, GEORGIA
191. Ermira Mitre Kokomani - CLIFTON, NEW JERSEY
195. Judy DeCroce - NEW YORK STATE
197. Antoni Ooto - NEW YORK STATE
201. Gary Shulman - PALM SPRINGS, CALIFORNIA
205. Nate McCall - SALEM, OREGON
209. Nila Bartley - OHIO
211. Mark O. Decker - OCEAN VIEW, DELAWARE

FRIENDS
noun

a person attached to another by feelings of affection
or personal regard.

a person who is on good terms with another;
a person who is not hostile.

FRIENDSHIP
noun

the state of being a friend; association as friends.

to value a person's friendship.

a friendly relation or intimacy.

friendly feeling or disposition.

www.Dictionary.com

Mark Saba

OLD GREENWICH, CONNECTICUT

Mark has been writing fiction, poetry, and creative non-fiction for 40 years. His book publications include, most recently, *Two Novellas: A Luke of All Ages/Fire and Ice* and *Calling the Names* (poetry), and *Ghost Tracks* (stories about Pittsburgh, where he grew up). His work has appeared widely in literary magazines around the USA, and abroad. Also a painter, Mark works as a medical illustrator at Yale University.

E: msaba@snet.net
W: www.marksabawriter.com
FB: @mark.saba.779

LETTER TO MY CHILDHOOD BEST FRIEND

I've been meaning
I've been meaning to
I've been really meaning to -

Oh, to so many things. Meaning to make progress;
to move on, up, around. Meaning to stop
feeling sorry for myself, or others.

Meaning to weed out my clothes
meaning to read a stack of books
meaning to tell my wife I love her.

Meaning to reach out to my siblings
meaning to hug my grown children
to teach them before it's too late.

Meaning to have a party and invite
so many friends.
Meaning to become an activist, to awaken

with more resilience. Meaning to empty myself
of all honours, qualifications, credentials.
Meaning to get in touch, to recover

fifty missing years. But all I do
is wonder if I will ever see such perfection
as those two ten year-olds sitting at the kitchen table

gluing model parts together
and seeing those finished get-away cars,
those metallic painted simulacra

of adult adventure, not knowing
we would be forever glued together
as the unknowns of adolescence, young adulthood,

parenthood, and now middle age
passed us by, with all those things
we were meaning to do.

Susan Vespoli
PHOENIX, ARIZONA

Susan lives in a 1970 ranch house with her two rescue dogs and, a couple nights a week, her granddaughter. She attended MFA school after she turned 50, loves to ride her bike, and has been published in spots such as *Rattle, Nasty Women Poets Anthology, Mom Egg Review, dancing girl press*, and others.
E: susan_vespoli@yahoo.com
FB: @susanvespoli

ON THE ONE-YEAR ANNIVERSARY OF YOUR EXIT

Because I didn't want to miss you, I cut
my hair and saged the house. Because I didn't want
to miss you, I dragged the futon mattress you slept on

that last night to the curb. Because I didn't want
to miss you, I heaped every flavor of Tillamook
onto a nightly cone, sometimes two, then I licked

them. Because I didn't want to miss you, I rode my bike
hundreds of laps around neighborhood blocks. Note: I
still ring that little round silver bell on the handlebars

you brought back from Japan. Because I didn't want to miss
you, I emptied my cupboards of all the dishes we'd dined on
and bought new ones, plus trashed the candles you'd lit.

Because I didn't want to miss you, I tore off our bed sheets
and bought a pink set. Because I didn't want to miss you,
I Goodwilled all my clothes you liked and kept the ones

you didn't, rolling your eyes, "you're still wearing THAT?"
Because I didn't want to miss you, I closed my eyes and chanted
OM to blank out your face. Because I didn't want to miss you,

I put photos of you and us in a bottom drawer, face down,
where I also shoved that post-it note you wrote and tacked
on my bulletin board. *My Susan, she can fly*. And then you drew a
heart.

FERRY RIDE

Crazy about ripples and light bouncing off
the surface of Puget Sound. Crazy about John

who spots seals bobbing like humans in swim caps,
points to a silvery blue-grey curved back

and tail that swoops above the water line,
says: "A whale!" as the ferry captain booms

over a loudspeaker, "Orcas at the bow!"
 and the passengers rise from their perches

to swarm the deck as the orca tucks itself back
under the water. And the throng in wool caps and hoodies

and raincoats wave their phones in the air,
shouting, "Where? Where? Where?"

ELECTRICITY IS THE PRESENCE AND FLOW OF ELECTRIC CHARGE

2007

Blue jeans, blue eyes, black shirt, straight teeth: you smile
at me in Pepe's booth. I grin at you.
You hold your hand out, take a breath, say, "Susan?"
I nod and touch your palm, then blush (I'm shy)
as currents, ohms, and voltage from you fly
into my fingers. Fire! Sparks! I swoon
as mariachis circle us with tune.
We order margaritas, chips. You buy.

2017

Flash forward ten years: you walk through the door
like clockwork, toss your shoes, drape clothes on chair,
ask, "How's your day?" with offhand glance at me
who sits on sofa watching you cross floor
to put your arms around me, touch my hair,
then ZAP I feel it: electricity.

Todd Matson
NORTH CAROLINA

Todd is a Licensed Marriage and Family Therapist. His poems, *All Diagnoses and Degrees Aside, When the Sheep Cry Wolf, Method to the Madness*, and *Pastor-Parish Relations* have been published in *The Journal of Pastoral Care & Counselling*; his poem *In Dreams* was published in the *Academy of the Heart and Mind*; his poem *The Gerrymanderer* has been published in *Bluepepper*; and his poem *Someone Please* has been published in *Love in the Time of Covid*. He has also written lyrics for songs recorded by number of contemporary Christian music artists, including *Forever,* by the Gaither Vocal Band; *Seasons of My Soul*, by Brent Lamb; *Heartsound*, by Connie Scott; and he co-wrote the lyrics for *When I Found You*, with contemporary Christian music artist, poet and author, Gloria Gaither. His short stories have been published in *Vital Christianity, Ariel Chart International Literary Journal, CaféLit, The Chamber Magazine, Literary Yard and Children, Churches & Daddies*.
E: tmatson4@hotmail.com

SECRET SAUCE

Start with a black, brown,
white, yellow or red person.

Add equal parts of...

empathy and compassion;
understanding and truth;
kindness and encouragement;
honesty and loyalty;
initiative and responsiveness;
mutuality and reciprocity;
vulnerability, laughter and tears;
quality time, affection and love.

Mix until trust becomes strong.

Gently blend in equal parts of...

a willingness to apologize when wrong;
a willingness to forgive when wronged;
a willingness to take a bullet not meant
for you.

Season generously with comic relief.

Enjoy for a lifetime.

Secret to the sauce: Use only organic
and natural ingredients, nothing artificial,
or your friendship will fall flat and spoil
quickly.

For a fun and satisfying variation,
start with something furry.

NOOSES AND LIFELINES

Too old for toys,
too young to drive,
bored out of our minds,
in serious need of adventure,
we took the nooses from
around our necks –
the ones we made from hemp
imported from Colombia
fashioned to end
our post-childhood misery.
We turned our nooses into lifelines.
We went tree-hopping –
me and my best friend,
both of us suspended
in young adolescent limbo,
each of us a cross between
Tarzan and Cheeta.
We started swinging and
jumping from tree to tree
around a grove of pine trees
as big as a city block.
The name of the game –
to make it around
the entire perimeter together
without hitting the ground.
Contact with the earth
meant you were dead.
Though we never
made it all the way around
the entire perimeter,
we went further together
than either of us
could have ever gone alone.
We took more leaps of faith
than we ever imagined taking.
We fell through pine needles
and broken branches
more times than we could count.
We hung on for dear life,
bruised and bleeding,
time and time again,
with our only lifelines being

the ropes we threw out
to each other,
the hands we reached out
to each other.
We lived and died
countless times together
when we were
suspended in limbo,
between times.

Joan McNerney
RAVENA, NEW YORK

Joan's poetry is found in many literary magazines such as *Seven Circle Press, Dinner with the Muse, Poet Warriors, Blueline,* and *Halcyon Days*. Four Bright Hills Press anthologies, several *Poppy Road* Journals, and numerous *Poets' Espresso Reviews* have also accepted her work. She has four Best of the Net nominations. Her latest title is *The Muse in Miniature.*
E: poetryjoan@statetel.com

SWEET COMFORT

For Sharon who sends amazing gifts and is amazingly gifted.

After eating three cookies, memories
of being twenty years old surround me.
Light bright dazzling, so fast, so sure
on high heels hurrying to work.
He ran but couldn't catch up. Another
one of those out-of-towners.

Now fifty years later, I should decide
what actually must be done on my LIST.
Would rather collapse on the couch.
Stare out the window. Better yet sink
into bed. Lie down blissfully and
reflect on life with all its zig zags.

Yet I must get up try to conquer just
one chore of dreaded housework.
Cookies beckon me. Three real
buttery spicy sugar cookies.
I surrender to this sweet magic,
soothing a cascade of years.

LOVE'S EQUATION
For Michael

Hope the phone bill isn't too high.
All he did last week was call
me from out of town.

Today he finally came home with
three red roses so I made him
twelve blueberry muffins.

For hours we kissed under moonlight
touching his mouth with my tongue ...
that electric tongue.

I put his two suitcases away
telling him to please be careful
with my clean floor.

Maybe one million times
I've told that man not to
make such as mess!

After twenty years, who's counting?

Norman Cristofoli

CANADA

Norman has published several chapbooks of poetry/prose, plus two audio compilations of spoken word. He published the *Labour of Love* literary magazine and co-founded the *Coffeehouse* artist networking site. His play *The Pub* and new book of poetry *Relinquishing the Past* were both published in 2020.

E: norman.cristofoli@gmail.com
W: www.normancristofoli.com

FRIENDSHIP APPLICATION

Don't need to know your name
Don't need to know your number
Just let me see your soul
Let me reach in and measure your heart
I want to see what is under
the masks that you wear

I'll want references from past friends
It would be in your favour
if you had been friends with Gandhi,
Martin Luther King, John Lennon,
Mother Teresa and Joan of Arc

You will need to give me
the definitive definition of friendship
Tell me what it means
Tell me where your heart lies
Where your loyalty is
Where you integrity is

Now, as it states in the application form
this is not a binding contract
I do not require advanced notice
if you're gonna split
after you've gotten what you come for

For my friendship is gold
My friendship is honest and pure
Filled with honour and respect
Too few have been worthy
Many have lured me with intellect
and discourses on spirituality
They only wanted to take and use
When nothing was left, they quickly disappeared
Some were actually in need,
in peril, in desperation
and I nursed their souls and hearts
Nursed their minds and their pocketbooks
Some even said "thanks" before they left

I don't mind the knife wounds
but at least bind the wounds afterwards

Nolo Segundo
MOORESTOWN, NEW JERSEY

Nolo Segundo is the pen name of L.J. Carber, Nolo only became a published poet as he neared his 8th decade, but has since had poems in published 35 literary magazines in the USA, UK, Canada, Romania, and India. In 2020, a trade publisher released a collection of his work titled *The Enormity Of Existence,* and in 2021 another collection titled *Of Earth and Ether.* Fifty years ago Nolo almost drowned in a Vermont river, and had a near-death experience which shattered his former faith in materialism; the idea that reality is only matter. He went from seeing life as meaningless, to knowing that the real problem was that there was so much meaning in everything - every action, every thought, every feeling. Being aware he has – is - a soul, an endless consciousness, may have helped him cope with teaching in the war zone of Cambodia, 1973-74 [leaving there about a year before the Killing Fields began]. He went on to teach ESL in Taiwan [where his wife is from] and Japan.
E: nolosegundo70@gmail.com

ODE TO MRS. MILLER

I did not know how brave she was —
Ninety-two and I, seventy less,
So young that old age
Was textbook stuff:
A fact of life,
But not mine.

I was alive and free
To stride the world,
A colossus of youth —
Whereas she had ate
Almost a century.
And all her friends
And all her family
Lay dead somewhere —
Except in her mind,
Still crisp, poignant
In its memories
Of a wealthy husband,
A daughter dead young.
Her own youth and beauty
Remaining lonely in a
Silver-framed photo.

She never complained,
This old lady —
Never once did I hear
Lamentations, a bewailing
For the richness of life:
The ripe fullness she once felt
As a wife, a mother, a woman
Of grace and beauty.

She lived alone
In a basement flat,
Barely five feet tall —
Yet I've never known
Any being braver —
Yet it is only now,
That I am become old,
I envy such courage.

Robert Beveridge
AKRON, OHIO

Robert makes noise and writes poetry, and his recent/upcoming appearances are in *Page and Spine, The Pointed Circle*, and *Failed Haiku*, among others.
E: xterminal@gmail.com
W: www.xterminal.bandcamp.com
W: www.last.fm/user/xterminal
Instagram: @ebolaisthesavior
Diaspora: @shorturl.at/pqzRV

IN TRANSITION

What is trust? In this
India ink night, I feel
your breath on my neck
and know you are
still beside me. Yet
when I stretch out
my arms, I encounter
only air. You set
my wings on fire,
though just my wings,
send them to nubs,
to scars that vanish
when you kiss me.

Your body this open
flame, this black flame,
this flame that seals
shut the walnut's shell
that contains the ashes
of neck, wings, tongue,
the wax from the candles
on my last cake. Fingers
burn, point to where
they believe you lurk,
where they believe you
bury your dead
in their shells, celebrate
until you join them

GIALLO

"Turn these stones to bread", you
challenge. I have, however, eaten
the flesh of earlier obsessions. Sated,
I have no reason to do anything but
pick up a stray bone, sharpen it, write.

A manta skates through the room despite
a distinct lack of water. The entire
party watches it, laconic, sips drinks,
then returns to their conversations
as if nothing untoward had occurred.

A friend of mine keeps a skull on his desk
at home. Says it helps him to write when he
stares his favourite critic in the face. We down
shots of chili purée backed with Old Ezra 103,
leave a pair for the skull, pick up our notebooks.

I'm not sure how he did it but the short
order cook at the greasiest spoon in North
East Philadelphia managed to make
the scrambled eggs match the colour of your
hair in a way Toulouse-Lautrec would envy.

We whispered down Spring Garden — no.
Stumbled. Sang the Nicene Creed in two
languages through hands we thought would
hold onto one another forever, hands
as slippery as the necks of our favourite bottles.

Phyliss Merion Shanken

ATLANTIC CITY, NEW JERSEY

Phyliss is a retired psychologist, playwright, and creative writing teacher, who has been published in psychological journals, literary publications, and weekly newspaper and magazine columns. In addition to her literary and poetry awards, she is author of *Silhouettes Of Woman* and *Peanut Butter Sandwich: The Joys and Frustrations of Parenting*, as well as a number of stage and screenplays. She has two novels, *Eye Of Irene*, and *The Heart Of Boynton Beach Club*. *Conversations With Perfect Strangers: Memoirs of a Psychologist* is the culmination of her life's work. She has been published in *Dreamers Creative Writing; The Write Launch, Abstract Contemporary Expressions, Non-Conformist Magazine, Beyond Words, Scarlett Leaf Review, Sad Girls Club Literary Blog, Catchwater Magazine, Fahmidan Journal, Pure Slush, Quillkeepers Press, Open Door Magazine*, among others … A number of her plays have been produced, the latest to be presented by Equity Library Theatre of NY.
E: pshanken@comcast.net
FB: @phyliss.shanken

T'AI

There are many fish in our sea.
Ahead of the rest, lighting our way,
swirls an iridescent one: see how
he swims beneath the nurturing pool.

He eats only plants.
He would not ingest a fellow fish,
for he is a gentle one who listens
to bubbles we make in his midst.
Sharks mellow when he is near,
and he sings his empathic song
to the weakest fishes who flutter about.

Steadfast in his countenance,
he takes many forms:
Angelfish, Goldfish, Sunfish.
He is a whale of a man.
Some days, a starfish he is.
We nose about him,
hoping to catch a glimpse of his beam.
Our tails fumble about for just one touch.

Imbibing our passions,
he melts humours we cloister within our being.
We are drunk from his wit.
We bottle his laughs and fold in his portrait,
now frozen in time.

The cool water, having been his native womb,
turns against him, seeping into his mass,
where it wants to linger without end.
Phosphorescent beads spurt from his chest,
as the minutes strike seven.
Our hearts cast infinite lines to him.
Though he holds us in his breath, he backslides
down, down, down a forbidding abyss.

He is snatched from his watery homeland,
we pray, to breath again.
But, having laid his hand on our souls,
while we swim in the tears of his memory,
he gracefully slips away.

TO ELEANOR

You said a word: I overheard it.
The echo bellows again:
Operation, Right Away, Emergency
Tomorrow, Biopsy, Serious, Biopsy
I am not afraid.
I watched a crystal inch along your face,
Like canvas, your cheek held it in a fairy tale.
Though you knew not of it, that was the moment we met.
I saw you from the distance, my own wells
brimming beneath a brilliant fire.
I peer at you on the ground of a mount
you have already climbed, I fear our finger tips
will never know the moisture of each other's dew.
I will look for God in your eyes;
I will search for the eyes of your twin
in all that I meet.
Woman, my human prayers cry helpless,
cry helpless, in the night.
There are more ridges
yet to be carved in your face.

Margaret Duda
STATE COLLEGE, PENNSYLVANIA

Margaret has had her work published in the *Kansas Quarterly*, the *Michigan Quarterly Review*, the *University Review*, the *South Carolina Review*, the *Green River Review*, *Crosscurrents, Fine Arts Discovery, Venture*, and the *Silver Birch Press*. One of her short stories made the Distinctive List of Best American Short Stories. She is now working on the final draft of a novel, and more poems.
E: mduda@ceinetworks.com

THE LONE RANGER

He was my best friend in our small town.

Two years older than my eight years, his
stringy red hair, thick dark-rimmed glasses,
and constant stutter made him a target for bullies,
forcing him to play with the girl next door.
I always insisted on being the Lone Ranger
and he had to settle for being my sidekick Tonto,
who called me Kemo Sabe, "faithful friend."
He let me wear the black mask and cowboy hat,
shoot rustlers with the silver bullets
in our pretend guns, and shout "Hi Yo, Silver"
as we galloped away after every adventure.

Without warning, his father was transferred,
his family moved away, and he galloped
out of my life.

Years later, after a lecture in New York City,
I heard "Hi Yo, Silver" from the crowd
amidst the squawking horns of cabs and
Tower of Babel dialects. I turned and barely
recognized Tonto wearing contacts and
a tailored suit befitting the manager of a
major Savings and Loan. He couldn't believe
it was really me and invited me to lunch,
where I discovered he overcame his stutter
as he showed me photos of his model-thin wife,
two perfect children, a house in the Hamptons.
Finally, he told me he thought of me often,
insisting I made his childhood bearable.

I should have let him be the Lone Ranger.

Jill Clark
DAYTONA BEACH, FLORIDA

Jill writes prose and poetry for children and adults, and is Children's Educational Specialist for Taylor and Seale Publishing. Her children's poetry book *Where Do Balloons Land?* will be released in the fall of 2021 - the follow-up to her first book *Loose Balloons* published in 2019. She presents Zoom lesson plans to public schools. Jill is SCBWI's (Society of Children's Books, Writers & Illustrators) regional Volusia County, Florida online writer's critique group leader.
E: jillmorgan2020@Instagram.com
E: jillclark2write@twitter.com
W: www.jillswriterscafe.com
FB: @LooseBalloons.jill.clark

WHO AM I?

I stand a little shorter than my classmates do.
But I am me, and you are you.
When I throw a baseball,
I wince and make a face,
the ball spins 'round and 'round, then drops in place.
I don't run fast or dribble a basketball well,
but in playful dance … I do excel.
I know the kids who need a friend, they are just like me—
shyer than the average kid but who LOVE to see
sunsets through the clouds as we listen to the waves.
We talk about the planets and explore hidden caves.
Rock-hunting in the mountains is just as much fun,
as watching my good friend make a homerun.
I love to hear my friend
thwack a grand slam,
I love me, too,
for who I am.

Dany Gagnon

CANADA

Dany is a game publisher, translator, and writer. After spending her formative years in London, England, she now lives in Montréal. She publishes poems in both English and French. Her works strive to describe the workings of our minds at the beginning of the 21st century. Since 2020, her poems have appeared in half of a dozen publications, at a DVAA group exhibition, and at a Parcours de la Poésie (poetry circuit).
E: danygagnon2019@icloud.com

BIRTHDAY FROM BEYOND

it will be my friend's birthday soon
we did not have much in common
but the one thing -
we were both shunning feeling pain
so much juice can be harnessed
from aching hearts -
we drank away till your last day

I've stopped running and dived into
fears losses and my loneliness
should you be here
we would not have much in common
freed as I am from my sadness
but then again
our bacteria have coupled

Happy Birthday
parts of you linger in my core

Cordelia Hanemann
RALEIGH, NORTH CAROLINA

Cordelia is currently a practising writer and artist. A retired professor of English at Campbell University, she has published in numerous journals including *Atlanta Review, Connecticut River Review, Dual Coast Magazine*, and *Laurel Review,* anthologies: *The Well-Versed Reader, Heron Clan* and *Kakalak,* and in her own chapbook *Through a Glass Darkly*. Her poem, *photo-op* was a finalist in the Poems of Resistance competition at Sable Press, and her poem *Cezanne's Apples* was nominated for a Pushcart. Recently the featured poet for Negative Capability Press and *The Alexandria Quarterly*, she is now working on a first novel, about her roots in Cajun Louisiana.
E: korkimax@gmail.com

FINDING RICHARD: AN ELEGY

The golden boy is gone,
has been gone a long time.
The setting of the sun over the Bay,
its golden glow at Richard's funeral.

> A boy, full of the glow of life, running
> and playing, playing tricks, fighting
> and shouting and laughing as boys do,
> a golden time. Your favourite childhood friend.

The funeral was fine, memorable,
Lafayette Park where Richard gardened
to support his art, which he could not sell,
wouldn't sell, old man hoarding his treasures.

In splintered light, his sculptures - faceless golems -
rescued and arrayed for ritual, for celebration,
gifts to friends who wanted them, gifts to the universe,
sentinels at attention - black, sombre, a little grotesque.

On the porch back home, on a spare stem of the potted plant,
itself bereft of leaves, a lone chrysalis, a Monarch,
glowing in its own potential future - a golden umbra
pulsing with the promise of new life, changing.

> Richard so handsome at 16, sharing his dreams -
> of art, of nature, of life, the escalating nightmares,
> stalked by dark creatures ready to devour,
> gnawing at his heart, his brain, something not right.

> Richard the gardener, digging and planting, planning
> imposing order, intuition, imagination like the sculptor
> bringing forth new life from fertile soil, as from virgin stone,
> the artist giving thought, touching, shaping - the fineness of the
>   lines.

> Richard hiding in the mystery of his golems, embryonic forms
> to which he gave birth, smaller than life and darker, stark,
> smooth, taking shape under his hand in his lonely space,
> then, rendering ugly what should be beautiful.

> Richard slathering his works with plaster, painting them black,

black as though too perfect for life. Erasing their faces, making
fraught what should protect and save, losing himself -
no identification, no identity - in the chrysalis of his apartment.

You had knocked on the door, promised to be the friend you'd
    always been,
but he could not let you in to the chaos he'd made unendurable,
un-sharable, his darknesses closing in, the door closed
against light, against you, against hope, against salvation.

At the park: five black sentinels arrayed in a line like a gauntlet,
his own sculptures abandoned by the hand that made them,
in the glow of the sunset - the words, the wine, the farewells,
car doors slamming, caravans driving back to lived lives.

You search your memory for that boy with his dreams,
with his nightmares, with his laughter and shouts,
his silences, those dark frowns, those runnings-away,
whom you could not help, could not save.

Richard: the part of you now lost. In the garden - the golems left
standing - what to do with them, the unwanted -
the friends having gone, the view, the wine and the words,
the sun going down into the Bay.

Back at the house the chrysalis has stopped, its glow
diminished, turned brown, then black, that little struggling life.
You reach out thinking of the life he had, the life he lost,
what you lost, the cold chrysalis in your hand,

Which you lay gently on the soil of the potted plant - a ritual of grief.

LEAVING: THE EDGE OF WINTER

And all the lives we ever lived and all the lives to be
Are full of trees and changing leaves. Virginia Woolf

It is the winter of our new year.
Withered Christmas trees hug the roadside.
Tangles of dry and leafless vines strangle tree limbs.
On the dull surface of the lake, a lone white gull floats.

Spare sun, shadows of weather everywhere,
The hues of a winter sky waiting for snow.
The last red leaves hold on before the coming freeze.
Beeches cling to crisp ecru leaves.

Yet sparkling green mosses creep up gnarly trunks,
and small glittering lichens spring from leaf piles;
Mahonia are ready to burst into flower, tiny yellow buds in spiky
        stars,
The camellia, weighed down with the pink froth of too many blooms.

My old friend - her smile despite recurring cancer -
And I - walking side by side, breathing.

Caroline Johnson
CHICAGO, ILLINOIS

Caroline has two illustrated poetry chapbooks *Where the Street Ends* and *My Mother's Artwork*, and more than 400 poems in print. A nominee for the Pushcart Prize and Best of the Net, she has won numerous national poetry awards, including the 2012 Chicago Tribune's Printers Row Poetry Contest. Her poetry was twice featured on Garrison Keillor's *Writer's Almanac*. A former English teacher, she is a college advisor and president of Poets & Patrons of Chicago, and has led workshops for veterans and other poets on such topics as Poetry and Spirituality, Speculative Poetry, and Writing About Chicago. Her full-length collection of poems, *The Caregiver* (Holy Cow! Press, 2018), was inspired by years of family care-giving.
E: carolinejohnson.author@gmail.com
W: www.caroline-johnson.com
FB: @carolinejohnsonauthor
Twitter: @twinkscat

GHAZAL FOR BRENDA

Oh God, the beautiful rose that You gave me,
I am giving back, but don't forget this weight, me.

The olives my Beloved and I picked on Easter Sunday,
no longer taste the same, no longer captivate me.

Oh! How I wish I could squeeze one in the palm of my hand,
then eat of the strange fruit that used to satiate me.

But I am drunk, sitting in the garden with wine and wild roses
instead of seeking the Beloved and His love that awaits me.

Why am I wasting time in the endless dark shadows
when like gold, You could transform and awaken me?

A breeze wakes up the skittery brown birds that sing,
resting on the barren cypress boughs that betray me.

Oh Brenda, learn from a worthless beggar such as me!
I only taste the olives. The fruit of suffering elates me.

THE FIGHT

Hot tears of lava spew from volcano.
I run. My skin freckles from the sun.
The lava oozes, hardens. We dash
in different directions, then stand
on the cooling surface, glaring.

We hop away from each other like
skittish birds. All history, civilization
is erased. Now to create a new life,
shape shift. Rock metamorphosizes,
tilts. What was up now is down.

But I can hear the Sikh music, the meditation.
It calls my name like the turban you gave me.
What am I supposed to do with it?
Give it back? I have grown my hair too long,
my life too strong, to untie the Rishi knot

we both made so long ago. My long hair is my
gift to God. My last name is still Singh, a lion.
Many Sikhs have been tortured so we can be
free. Don't give up your religion, your soul.

The gurdwara is calling us to come together,
to pray once more. Why not leap out of the
volcano and meet me at the Doorway to the
Divine? Forget the heat, the angry words.
Listen to the singing. Let it lighten your life.

SHE SAYS BLUE LOOKS GOOD ON ME

As I sit across from her at Panera
measuring her huge brown eyes,

the brief cami shows some cleavage,
despite only one breast and a scar.

She says I look great, looking at my
new hair. I get into my car and merge

with traffic, wait to shift gears
and plow on, like a true soldier.

Charles Leggett
SEATTLE, WASHINGTON

Charles is a professional actor. His poetry has been published in the US, the UK, Ireland, Canada, Australia, New Zealand, Singapore and Nigeria, and in publications including *Magma Quarterly, Firewords Quarterly, The London Reader, Creative Writing Ink, As Above So Below, Constellate: A Literary Journal*, *Sylvia Magazine, Ocotillo Review, Sage Cigarettes, Volney Road Review, Heirlock Magazine, Automatic Pilot* and Poetica Publishing's latest *Mizmor Anthology.* Work is forthcoming in *Welter, The Hollins Critic*, and *Cheap Imitation*.
E: leggettcharles@hotmail.com

LETTER TO A FRIEND WITH A BLACK BELT

Your handwriting has all the arrogance
Of a kitten readying to heist
Some trifling thing that one might need, by chance:

His eyes depose with an unremitting glance
That he will steal one's pencil and be chased.
Your handwriting has all the arrogance

A postman ever wants to see your stamps
Upstaged by; using my real name (t's crossed)
- A niggling thing that you might wish, by chance,

To try and do - would somewhat more enhance
The odds of my getting mail, not, say, Chuck Leglost.
Your handwriting has all the arrogance

With which to eerily belie your dance,
Which isn't, and you smile as you protest,
Protection you may one day need, by chance,

But rather your salvation, your new pants,
Your cult of energy, of love, of test.
Your handwriting has all the arrogance,
A small, fine thing that you may need, by chance.

Suellen Wedmore
ROCKPORT, MASSACHUSETTS

Suellen graduated from the MFA Program in Poetry at New England College in 2004, and is Poet Laureate emerita for the small seaside town of Rockport. She has been widely published, and awarded first place in the Writer's Digest's Rhyming Poem and Non-Rhyming Poem Contests. Her chapbook *Deployed* won the Grayson Press annual contest, her chapbook *On Marriage and Other Parallel Universes* was published by Finishing Line Press. and her chapbook *Mind the Light* won a first place in Quill's Edge Press's Women on the Edge contest. In 2014 she won first place in the Studios of Key West Contest, and three of her poems have been nominated for a Pushcart Prize.
E: suellenwedmore@comcast.net

POEM IN WHICH I IMAGINE GOD AS A BARTENDER

For Jane. & Carole, friends for thirty years

Not to complain, Lord, but this Time thing's a cheat—
while a minute goes down slow, like a shot of good gin,
the years blur into a barstool's spin.
It's all happening too fast, Lord! Now wouldn't it be sweet
to pour Time, neat like whiskey, into an uplifted glass,
round after round of tears and bite and sass?
Like summer settling on a Baby Boomer's dream,
whiskey with resonance of truth-telling, consistency of cream,
decanted for friends with a cheerful *Bottoms up*,
aperitif for chat, jokes and puns on tap!
Give me a cocktail that stifles gripes and groans,
a toast, *salud*, to health, another year on loan.
Don't cut me off, Boss. Believe me, I'm no trouble—
if "last call" is the end game … make my drink a double!

Michael H. Brownstein

JEFFERSON CITY, MISSOURI

Michael's latest volumes of poetry, *A Slipknot to Somewhere Else* (2018) and *How Do We Create Love?* (2019), were published by Cholla Needles Press.

E: mhbrownstein@ymail.com

MORNING WALK

I walk the cane corso early evening,
day slowly changes its clothing,
and he sees ghosts in the night shadows,
a cat, a squirrel, too often another dog.

Is it possible for day to put on a red dress?
Perhaps a pair of shiny flats? A strand of pearls?
What is it with these greys and blacks,
stripes, prints, patterns of invisibility?

The cane corso never sees any of that,
only his ghosts hiding in the doorways,
shadows within shadows, shades of black,
a grand silence of nothing stepping toward us.

Krikor Der Hohannesian
MEDFORD, MASSACHUSETTS

Krikor is of Armenian descent, his forebears having fled the Turkish genocide. His poems have appeared in over 175 literary journals including T*he Evansville Review, The South Carolina Review, Atlanta Review, Louisiana Literature, Connecticut Review, Comstock Review* and *Natural Bridge*. He is a three-time Pushcart Prize nominee, and the author of two chapbooks *Ghosts and Whispers* (Finishing Line Press, 2010) and *Refuge in the Shadows* (Cervena Barva Press, 2013), as well as a full-length book, *First Generation* (Dos Madres Press, 2020). *Ghosts and Whispers* was a finalist for the Mass Book awards poetry category in 2011.
E: krikorndh@verizon.net

SOUL BROTHER

We celebrated for three days,
chewed on stories, grooved with Paul Robeson,
Joe Cocker, Jimmy Cliff, Louis Armstrong,
got down and dusty on baby backs, collards,
dirty rice, sweet potato pie. Drowned the blues
in drink, raised the rafters with hallelujahs.

The day-after tears - not the choked back kind but
full-bore gushing – finally swamped me
like a rogue wave. I am lost,
marooned on an isle of mourning. Dusk
falls in silence, I grope the gloom
for solace, praying for grace. It is late fall -
a rising gibbous moon backlights skeletal maple,
the marigolds rust and wilt, squirrels rustle
leaves burying winter caches, fallen apples
rot to their cores, geese in v-formation
intent on climes more clement.

You shouldn't have left so soon, there are things
not finished. We were to be octogenarians together,
to be the wisest of the wise – wiser than Solomon,
filled with more stories than the eldest griot.

You shouldn't have left so suddenly, there
are things yet unsaid, inchoate raps in need
of ripening - never mind proper farewells.

Tomorrow's forecast is inclement. I shall write
your epitaph, as asked, and weep some more
in concert with the rain. In December days
perhaps the cold will numb but I will feel
mortality's sleety sting against a frozen face.

Come March, April the crocuses' yellows
and purples will not be quite so brilliant,
the grass shoots not quite so verdant,
the mockingbirds' trills and runs
a shade short of their usual bravura.
I shall dig holes for plantings nonetheless.

THE MOMENT

Somewhere you wait, silent
companion life-long at my elbow
in this rutted trek we share.
Make no mistake – I've
had it easy. I have loved
and been loved, belly never
knifed by starvation's pangs
nor psyche dealt the torment
of those wishing harm.
I have played and danced and sung,
laughed and wept, praised and cursed.

Yet this need to know you!
To see you as friend
not mysterious foe,
to imagine you under a cherry tree
as blood red fruit, fully ripe, falls
to your lap, to picture you lolling
on a deserted beach soaked
in the warmth of a July sun
rivulets of salt-blue high tide
washing over your feet - your smile
smug in knowing that you
have last dance.

How will you come to me?
A knocking at the door, soft
and undemanding or hard
and insistent? Guest at my table
or unwanted intruder? Or will
I come to you? This

I cannot know. I can but pray
we lock arms when
the moment is upon us
to walk, not in dread,
but with wonder through
the black-veiled portal.

Kathy Sherban
CANADA

Kathy (Moorehead) Sherban is a poet and author of soon to be published *Accidental Poetess*. Her career as a Financial Controller and Compliance Consultant respectively spanned 35 years in Toronto's Stock Market. As a recent retiree her time is dedicated to writing poetry, reading books and planning future travel adventures.
E: kmsherban@gmail.com
FB: @kats_kradle
FB: @Kat's Poetry Korner
Instagram: @kat_s_kradle
Twitter: @kathysherban

COUNTERFEIT FRIEND

Into infinity
shallow words flow
Cascading covertly
ever so slow
Carried by wind
a stealthy dart
Deaf ears listen
targeting the heart
Absent candour
deficit is clear
Behind the veil
duplicity appears
Sincerity absent
lip service trends
Beyond the shadows
a counterfeit friend

BIRDS OF A FEATHER

Kindred spirits
trusted & true
Absent judgement
right on cue
Ears to listen
hearts that share
Smiles to brighten
people who care
Inside jokes
one of a kind
Pillar of strength
inspirational mind
Straight shooter
honest to a fault
Leads with integrity
designed to exalt
Birds of a feather
soft place to land
Lifetime journey
outstretched hand
Gestures of friendship
year after year
Bonded forever
time disappears

CHOSEN ONES

Inner circle
solidarity grows
Pedigree blends
trust bestowed
Comrades chosen
allegiance sworn
An eternal bond
family formed
Kindred spirits
sign from above
Flawed humans
imperfect love
God's gift
inside voice
Friends turned family
always a choice

Jan Ball
CHICAGO, ILLINOIS

Jan started seriously writing poetry and submitting it for publication in 1998. Since then, she has had 336 poems accepted and/or published in the U.S., Australia, Canada, India, Ireland, Czech Republic and England. Published poems have appeared in *ABZ, American Journal of Poetry, Calyx, Chiron, Main Street Rag, Phoebe* and many other journals. Her poem *carwash*, won the 2011 Betsy Colquitt Award for the best poem in a current issue of *Descant, Fort Worth*. More recently, Jan's poem *Loquat Jam* was awarded first place in the annual Loquat Festival of Port Ritchie, Florida (2018). Her poem *Not Sharing at Yoshu* was nominated for the Pushcart by *Orbis Literary Review* (2020, England). Her three chapbooks, *Accompanying Spouse* (2011), *Chapter of Faults* (2014), and *Day Job* (2020) have been published by Finishing Line Press, as well as her first full length poetry collection *I Wanted To Dance With My Father* (2017). Jan is a member of The Poetry Club of Chicago, and besides her poetry publications, she wrote a doctoral dissertation at the University of Rochester in 1996 titled *Age and Natural Order in Second Language Acquisition,* did undergraduate work at Alverno College and DePaul University and, most recently, taught ESL at DePaul University in Chicago.
E: janiceball@usa.net

CAROLYN

No more bouffant blonde wigs,
no more business jackets cinched
at the waist, forty-two-year-old
Carolyn lies dying, morphined
at home and bald like she never
was at Philadelphia dinner parties,
with her dramatic gestures and
Julia Roberts smile. A distraught
son stands crying in a corner of
the unlit kitchen once Thanksgiving
festive; a long daughter stretches
like a devoted cat on the other side
of the blue chenille bedspread.

I asked my anaesthesiologist friend
who is accustomed to death what
I should say when the call came:
You'd better go immediately if you
want to say goodbye, a co-incidence
that I was in town for a conference.
Pam drove me to the darkened house
in the cul-de-sac where they live. As
she suggested, I said, *Carolyn,*
the moon is bright tonight. It smells
like winter, then let go of her hand
when I realized she couldn't hear me.

At the bottom of the stairs, I held
her husband tightly, glad that I
worked out Mondays and Thursdays,
so firmly did he cling to me as he
sobbed into my hair like a frightened
child, *I can't do it; I can't do it.*
I said, *Oh, yes you can*, as I walked
out the door to catch my plane.

MARGIE AND THE MENNONITE

We've seen the women in high-neck
summery dresses and lace caps waiting
for the bus when we drive past en route
to downtown Sarasota.

Once we shared our table at Starbucks
with an amiable person who we think
was an Amish man: blue shirt, black pants,
a bicycle leaning against a tree and then,
of course, *Witness* with Harrison Ford
punching the bully.

Now, my friend, Margie, says that she
has finally found a new companion
after her husband, Rod, died seven years
ago.

The new guy is Mennonite, she says, but he
drinks wine and worked in a micro-biology
lab with her, that's how she got to know him.

Regardless of what her children think, she
has sold her suburban house to move in
with him on his Wisconsin farm.

We haven't seen Margie in many months,
passing like two ships in the night, my folks
used to say, so arrange to meet her
at the Chinese Restaurant we used to go to
with her and Rod.

Margie calls two days before our planned
dinner and says, "John wants to meet my friends;
he's coming, too," so we change the reservation.

I already know what I'm going to order: turnip
dim sum and hot and sour soup.

We get there first so ask for the table
in the quiet alcove with a view of downtown
Chicago where we used to sit with Margie and Rod.

Margie and John arrive and he looks normal:
nice leather jacket, short greying hair, no blue
shirt, suspenders or straw boater. I don't get
to look at his shoes.

Soon after they sit down, John says,
"I'm a Mennonite. There's a big range
in practices among us."

As we talk, he tells us that when he was drafted
into the army from his Dad's Central Illinois farm,
he declared conscientious objector status,

I think, "like the guy in Mel Gibson's
Hacksaw Ridge." The army trained him
in a medical field, as they do with conscientious
objectors so he didn't have to touch a gun.

For the rest of the night, as I look through
the steam of my hot and sour soup, I try
to introduce a variety of topics: gay marriage,
racism and equal pay for equal work.

Google has warned me that these are
hot topics for Mennonites but either the fish
does not rise to the bait or we can't believe
everything Google says.

Linda M. Crate
MEADVILLE, PENNSYLVANIA

Linda's works have been published in numerous magazines and anthologies, both online and in print. She is the author of six poetry chapbooks, the latest of which is *More Than Bone Music* (Clare Songbirds Publishing House, March, 2019). She's also the author of the novel *Phoenix Tears* (Czykmate Books, June, 2018). Recently she has published two full-length poetry collections *Vampire Daughter* (Dark Gatekeeper Gaming, February, 2020), and *The Sweetest Blood* (Cyberwit, February, 2020).
E: veritaserumvial@hotmail.com

THANK YOU FOR BEING A FRIEND

i haven't heard for you
for a long while,
but thank you for being there
for me during the roughest
period of my life;

thank you for taking my side
and recognizing that my ex
was a terrible person -

so many people told me he
was a good man,
but he left me in shambles
after his false sincerity and all his lies
my exhaustion was immense;

but you listened to me and helped me
through the mire he left me in

i will forever appreciate that
more than you could possibly know
because instead of taking the side
of one of your fellow men,

you supported the woman broken
by him.

SOME BONDS CANNOT BE BROKEN

every visit
we have

i learn that we have
something else
in common,

guess that's why we're
best friends;

we even have the same
zodiac sign and our birthdays
are eight days apart -

introverts that are dreaming
of adventure,

finding fun in so many different forms:
everything from museums to boat rides
to nature walks and walks in the wood -

so much love and laughter
weaves us together

the stars of our galaxies will always
recognize the souls
we are

because some bonds cannot be broken.

YOU'RE THERE FOR ME ALWAYS

you listened to me cry on the phone
without judgment,

you were there for me when i thought
i was going to fall apart;

you were there for me when my family
was being terrible to me -

you were there when i didn't know
how to go on

encouraging and loving me even when
i was a weepy, self-destructive mess;

and when i was able to find my joy again
you were there, too;

a true friend sticks with you through thick and thin &
you're there for me always.

APPEARANCE

Mantled with understatements,
after the years we see that

- not everything is as
we thought.
When we were needed
- they were with us.

Now
they don't waste time
- they leave.

Apparent, loyal friends
have their own plans.

CREASE

Is there any sense?
Maybe just for a try?

Resurrecting friendship
is like
filling a blown egg.
There will always be
a gap, void,
that
will not allow you to return
to the state it was before.

An attempt
may seemingly succeed,
but
the painful crease inside
will someday resurrect.

Laura Nagy
KAILUA KONA, HAWAI'I

Laura is a retired educator, writer, and editor who continues to explore the nexus of her two academic disciplines - literature and ecology - in her writing. Her journalistic work has been widely published, and her fiction and poetry have appeared in *Sounds, The Mill, The Main Street Rag, Bloodroot Literary Magazine*, and *Quintessence*. She was a Pushcart Prize nominee in 2014. She is currently completing a book on the history and ramifications of predator eradication in the American West during the late nineteenth and early twentieth centuries. She lives with her wife and two dogs in Kailua Kona, Hawai'i.

E: lnagy@wildcats.unh.edu

MAHOGANY MEMORIES

My lover's coat hangs by mine on the rack
on the café wall.
The room is all ours for now;
lunch is long done,
just kitchenward clatters of pots
and voices recapping
mealtime mayhem.
They'll leave us alone;
it's been our place
for so long now,
they know what we'll drink
before we do.

That first time, like first times,
the strangeness and wondering
drained all of the air from the room.
As I worked to draw breath
I hardened my heart for
the parting, like others before it,
all awkward and sad,
the stumbling away like a three-legged dog.
Yet,
when October light, suffused with gold
washed a silhouette into the just-opened door,
I had to look up
at the parcel of ramifications,
gilded by autumn's
bittersweet epilogue.

The parcel was you,
and we lingered long,
sipping wine in deepening dusk,
just as we do now.
Low-slung sun through smoky windows
backlights slatted chairs
and conjures mahogany memories.
We sit in calm silence—
we know what we'd say
if we chose to,
but know, too,
we don't really need to.
Instead, we lean back

to ruminate,
to savour the musky taste
on our tongues of a time
when love flowed as freely
as pinot does now.

FULL CIRCLE

I trim my mother's toenails
as we sit on my back stoop.
Brittle they are
and ragged as shagbark;
they're out of her reach -
back stiffened, girth grown,
replaced hip
replaced.
Bone erodes bone:
given enough years,
we wear ourselves
right down to dust.

Deepening dusk
conjures an image:
of her holding
my miniature fingers
a lifetime ago
in her own -
tiny pale crescents,
delicate cuts,
made with such
patience and care.
Things do go round,
and come back round, too,
full circle.

Now I sit two steps down
and cradle her heel in my lap
as I work.
We talk of nasturtiums,
dead uncles, ripe fruit,
and that day in Wyoming,
the dry prairie path
where a rattlesnake
coiled in brown grass
rasped at our feet.
The clippers snip, chips fly -
no other movement
this moment, it seems,
yet somewhere the Earth turns,
unseen.

As darkness descends
just then and just vague,
an arching, aching
evening breeze
curls complicit
through bent birch trees.
It bears a thought I've thought,
but never said,
and suddenly I say it:
"Mom,
I'll miss you so much when you're gone."
The clippers lie still in my palm.

She leans in and laughs,
kisses my head,
pats my hair
like she's dusting me off
and sending me back out to play
after tending to
skinned-knee catastrophe.
"Oh, no, you won't," she says,
and then smiles,
"because I'll come back
to haunt you."

Hanh Chau
SAN JOSE, CALIFORNIA

Born in Vietnam, of Chinese descent, Hanh has a Bachelor's and Master's degree in Business administration. During her spare time, she enjoys writing, listening to music and spending with her family.
E: hanhchau387@yahoo.com

A FRIENDSHIP ROSE BLOOM

A lovely radiant rose
You are my dearest friend
That I come to know
With the exquisite beauty
In the splendour view
Of the green growing field
With the soft petal touch
Of the blooming flourish
That never cease to exude
With its own vibrant colour
That you bring to share
With your uplifting spirit soul
And elegant poise smile
To bring hope and joy
Through the darkness time
A spectacular rosebud of
friendship that it grows
through the nurturing
of plant seed
like you and I form
to become a sisterhood
Despite of the bitterness cold
and stormy weather
it maintains survive
with the sharp prickle thorn
of its strength that symbolize
That it stands out from the crowd
Carry on with a gracious display kind
That embrace with sincerity
Through eternity

Ian Cognitō
CANADA

Ian is a poet from Vancouver Island. He is the author of three collections of poetry including *Animusings, Much Adieu about Nothing*, and *flora, fauna & h. sapiens* (the latter two, co-authored with Pat Smekal). Ian recently produced and edited an anthology on the topic of ageing (again with Pat), *Old Bones & Battered Bookends* unites poets from across Canada to explore this lofty topic in poetic form. This Fall, Ian will publish *Interchange*, a poetry/prose exchange with Ontario prose writer Anne Marie Carson. He is the producer/artistic director of *15 Minutes of Infamy*, a word-craft cabaret based in Nanaimo, BC, and runs an independent publishing company Repartee Press. Ian's previous incarnations have included language instructor, child and youth care-worker, and mask maker/clown.
E: repartee@telus.net
FB: @Reparteepress

LIFTED

on days
when you could just
curl yourself up
into a ball of grief
to mourn
each mounting loss:
the loved ones, gone
the missed opportunities
faculties that tumble
one by one
all the things you do
to keep yourself busy
while you await
your own turn
to relinquish
to loosen your grip
to un-pry
those fingers

on these days
what a simple smile
could do
offered up, placed just so
a genuine upturning
at the corners
of another's lips
someone
who knows
all too well
this
is not your day
to unfurl

someone
who's having
a better day

YOUR FINE EXAMPLE

I so admire
your ability to bring
a ritual quality
to seemingly mundane activities

In your hands
a task
as simple as making the bed
takes on a new significance
pillows fluffed
corners folded and tucked
each in its own turn
each as it must be

When you dress yourself
you take the time
to find the right combination
as if you're dressing
the mood of the moment
or your aspiration
for that day

When you clean your house
do laundry
wash the dishes
one does not sense
you are harnessed
to the drudgery
of some domestic chore
a compulsion
to sweep away
some hidden guilt
One senses instead
a desire for connection
as you move through each step
of each endeavour
with undivided attention

You imbue
everything you do
with symbolic import
embracing every moment

giving each undertaking
a deeper meaning
the power to transform
to connect you
with something rich
and powerful
within yourself

And I, of course
am beholden
to your fine example
though, I must admit
it has rubbed off
only superficially
I'm still in a hurry
to get nowhere in particular
as I wait for you
Here
at the finish line

Linda McCauley Freeman
HUDSON VALLEY, NEW YORK

Linda has been widely published in international literary journals and anthologies, including a Chinese translation of her work. Most recently she appeared in *Amsterdam Quarterly*, won Grand Prize in StoriArts poetry contest honouring Maya Angelou, and was selected by the Arts MidHudson for their Poets Respond to Art 2020 and 2021 shows. She was a three-time winner in the Talespinners Short Story contest judged by Michael Korda. She has an MFA in Writing and Literature from Bennington College, and is the former poet-in-residence of the Putnam Arts Council.
E: lmccfreeman@gmail.com
FB: @LindaMcCauleyFreeman

WE WERE YOUNG TOGETHER
Ode to Wayne 1960-2011

The boy in the white house, two
houses down, showed me
his blistered back, his father's strap.
He'd help me up the hill, then push me
down. Throw rocks at my head. Ring
doorbells and run.

Days became years became nights
my windows pebbled till I climbed out.
Crank calls he or she met at a bar,
Don't you remember? hang up, snorting
laughter and beer, hang out hours on my
porch steps or on the rusted lawn chairs
in his backyard. A Marlboro always
between his lips that never touched mine.
I'd watch the tip burn, the way he'd squint
when he drew the smoke in. We'd pass
warm vodka, kill time, use his long string
of girlfriends to drive us around.

I must have seen him in something other
than his brown leather jacket, tee shirt
and jeans, but that is all I remember. I can still
smell the jacket and cigarettes, see his yellow -
tinged fingers. I cried on his shoulder
over every boyfriend, he could be so gentle.
I have a photo of him taken in my bedroom,
holding my stuffed bear when we were too old
for such things. His eyes were blue, his hands
scraped from his garden. He always lit up
his father's house for Christmas, the festive
package wrapping the hell he lived within.
He never came to school. We never talked about
what was real, only his hypochondria, his certainty
of pending doom.

When I was away at college, he'd call, late
in my dorm, slurring words. But home, he was
always there in the white house. Now it was bars
and clubs instead of lawn chairs and steps. But it was
the same, even when he got his girlfriend pregnant,

even when they moved to Florida, even when I pointed
down the block to a visiting boyfriend saying,
that white house is where my friend, Wayne, lived ...
and stopped because it was yellow
and there were little kids playing out front.

He followed me long before Facebook,
through my two marriages, random late-night calls
until the one from his wife:
Wayne is dead. We're bringing him home ...

Wayne in the casket, looking like he just passed out.

WHO WE BECAME
For Wendy, Lisa, Peggy & Me

Can we see in the old photo
the women we became?
Was there prediction
in how one of us stands steady
head held high as her mother
drank herself to death and her
father was so old to us even then.
Was nurse prescribed to her as she
swaddled her baby brother,
a fragile boy I still remember?

How the four of us found
each other again on Facebook
after 40 years and still
knew each other intimately.
How one of us can finally
lift her head and smile
directly into the lens,
though her hair still hangs
over her small face
that creases with work and worry
but shines over photos
of her children and grandchildren.

And our beautiful girlfriend,
the one the other three
of us prayed to look like,
who married her high school
sweetheart who beat
her until she gathered
her child and strength
to leave him and how now
it is her goodness
and kindness that frames
the new photo of us four.

And how I am who I am
partly because of who
the four of us were together.

And how I still love these
girls and the women they became.

Mark Fleisher
ALBUQUERQUE, NEW MEXICO

Mark's writings have taken him around the world – his work has been published in numerous online and print anthologies in the United States, United Kingdom, Canada, Nigeria, Kenya, South Africa, and India. He has also published three volumes of poetry – with prose and photography added - titled *Moments of Time, Intersections: Poems from the Crossroads* and *Reflections: Soundings From the Deep*, and has collaborated on a fourth book *Obituaries of the Living*. Fleisher received a journalism degree from Ohio University. His service in the United States Air Force included a year as a combat news reporter in Vietnam, where he was awarded a Bronze Star for meritorious service.

E: markfleisher111@gmail.com
E: markfleisher333@gmail.com

ELEGY FOR STEWART

"Here he lies where he longed to be,
Home is the sailor, home from sea,
And the hunter home from the hill"
 - Robert Louis Stevenson

A shooting star sprinting across
our individual skies, slowing
to dock in mutual spaces
where he shared
the wisdom and warmth
of his words, always
with a sparkling smile
and twinkling eyes

Ever grateful for his encouragement
encapsulated in simplest terms
it's good, he'd say, as he
boosted your confidence while
whittling away at your doubt

His own words bathed in spirituality
flowing off the page, hearing
his voice in each syllable,
imagining the ineffable aura
he transmitted to all

Now, dear friend, the battle
is ended; let us applaud
your courage, admire
your fighting spirit

It is time

Go rest high on that mountain

McKenna Themm
SAN DIEGO, CALIFORNIA

McKenna is currently an MFA in Creative Writing: Poetry student at San Diego State University. Her poems have been published by *The San Diego Union-Tribune, JMWW, Bryant Literary Review, pacificREVIEW, Luna Luna* and *The Stray Branch*. She is writing her first full-length ekphrastic collection of poems based on the life and work of Vincent van Gogh. She is the managing editor at the *Los Angeles Review*, a Content Strategist at Archer Education, and the MFA Director's Assistant at SDSU.
E: mckennathemm@gmail.com
Instagram: @mckenna.themm
Instagram: @kenna.themm

HOW TO NOT FORGET
To Chandler

I try to memorize
the nightly migration
patterns of crows as they
gather like clouds to the

coast and frame the ocean
like a portrait, the same way
you pull on the collared rim
of your coat and it frames your

freckled cheeks. And my
restless feet cannot stay
grounded. Like butterflies, they
race toward the waves until

I melt into the warm sand and
allow the lapping constancy to
lull me into a rest
I have all but forgotten.

OVER AGAIN

"Painters understand nature and teach us to see."
Vincent van Gogh

Nature falls in love with herself
over and over again

for she understands that
       death is just a word that means
for now, we are separated

by some atmosphere. And she
       laughs through a series of monologues,
paint dripping from her fingers as her
conic clouds
pave the road upon which sparrows

fly. She falls - but not like water - as
she gives up the right to watch
       us, like bees to wildflowers,
       gather warmth and attempt to capture light
the way glass captures fingerprints.

For those who wait, she dances
as the tide unravels itself.

Over and over again
       she holds the hands of those
       who hold the universe
within their dimpled smiles.

TO MY SOULMATE

"If ever you fall in love, do so without reservation, or rather, if you should fall in love simply give no thought to any reservation."
Vincent van Gogh, 1881.

I have walked, pulse-quickening, in and out
of each of the
      four chambers,
a time or two,
every day to close all the doors with

care - mending, healing, as best I can.
But no matter how many times I turn
my back on your door,
      it remains open:

just a crack, just enough for a stream of
light to illuminate the particles
of dust drifting,
      dancing through the air. And

though I have eliminated the thought
of ever loving again the others who once
      occupied each deep corridor of my

heart, I keep your door ajar,
just in case
you happen to open it again,
step out, and find your way back to me.

Akua Lezli Hope
NEW YORK CITY

Akua is a creator and wisdom seeker who uses sound, words, fibre, glass, metal, and wire to create poems, patterns, stories, music, sculpture, adornments, and peace. She wrote her first speculative poems in the sixth grade, and has been in print every year - except one - since 1974. She is published in numerous literary magazines and national anthologies. A third generation New Yorker, her honours include the NEA, two NYFAs, an SFPA award, multiple Rhysling and Pushcart Prize nominations, among others. She twice won Rattle's Poets Respond. Her first collection *EMBOUCHURE, Poems on Jazz and Other Musics*, won the Writer's Digest book award. A Cave Canem fellow, her collection *Them Gone*, was published 2018. She launched Speculative Sundays, an online poetry reading series. She won editorship of *Nombono*, an anthology of BIPOC speculative poems to be published fall 2021 by Sundress Publications. She is the editor of the forthcoming issue of *Eye To The Telescope on the sea*. Her micro chapbook of *scifaiku, Stratospherics*, is in the Quarantine Public Library. Her chapbook, *Otherwheres* (ArtFarm Press 2020), is nominated for a 2021 Elgin award. She sings songs from her favourite anime in Japanese, practices her soprano saxophone, and prays for the cessation of suffering for all sentience from the ancestral land of the Seneca, the Southern Finger Lakes region of New York State.
E: akualezli@gmail.com
W: www.akualezlihope.com
Instagram: @AkuaLezliHope

SOMETIMES I STILL FORGET

Sometimes I still forget
this show is one you would like
the phone rings and I think it might be you

Last time we spoke, so much more to tell
my first flameworked beads, your quilting class
Sometimes I still forget

Calla lilies become, green folds turn sunshine
You gave me Hepburn, made me bloom
the phone rings and I think it might be you

Crocheted gold flowers fill the outline
Want your insight, need your advice
Sometimes I still forget

Figured out rice ice cream, planted lemon mint
decipher what you taught, replace the plants you brought
the phone rings and I think it might be you

Now grief thins, ebbs and flows
after twenty-three years of things to tell and show
Sometimes I still forget
when the phone rings and I think it might be you

UNREMEMBERED

I thought of the long-limbed girl with curly hair
laughing in my backyard. She has a ponytail.
I have bangs and my legs are folded under me
how I loved yoga taught by Richard Hittleman on Channel 13
in black and white, like the photo.
It is my birthday, there is a part down the middle
of my head and I have two cornrows tugging my short,
hot-comb straightened knots into neatness.
There is another girl on the grass,
smaller than both of us, the same age,
but less sprouted. I don't remember her.
I google the one I recall, her three-syllable name
becomes four in Italian, where it set Dante's heart aflame.
Her huge, dark father was a GI with a short war bride
Her mother taught me to use the abacus
my aunt had sent as a souvenir from Tokyo
on the large ebony and ivory one in her home,
an elegant and alien tool, musical, smooth -
I wanted to say how special it all seemed,
how I never forgot her last name, its honorific quality,
but she didn't remember me.
Nor did the boy I was smitten with
his bold red lips, ever ready grin, unruly curls
my father knew, my brother teased
in the time I didn't like boys.
He gave me one of his dog's puppies.
In his radical autobiography, the picture
of our bad Shag's collie-like dam is there,
as is one of our elementary school class
taken on a day I was absent.

First published in *WordGathering*, Volume 7, Issue I.

J.J. Steinfeld
CANADA

Canadian poet, fiction writer, and playwright J. J. Steinfeld lives on Prince Edward Island, where he is patiently waiting for Godot's arrival and a phone call from Kafka. While waiting, he has published 21 books, including *Misshapenness* (Poetry, Ekstasis Editions, 2009), *Identity Dreams and Memory Sounds* (Poetry, Ekstasis Editions, 2014), *Madhouses in Heaven, Castles in Hell* (Stories, Ekstasis Editions, 2015), *An Unauthorized Biography of Being* (Stories, Ekstasis Editions, 2016), *Absurdity, Woe Is Me, Glory Be* (Poetry, Guernica Editions, 2017), *A Visit to the Kafka Café* (Poetry, Ekstasis Editions, 2018), *Gregor Samsa Was Never in The Beatles* (Stories, Ekstasis Editions, 2019), and *Morning Bafflement and Timeless Puzzlement* (Poetry, Ekstasis Editions, 2020). A new poetry collection, *Somewhat Absurd, Somehow Existential*, is forthcoming from Guernica Editions in fall 2021.

NOT OF THE ETERNAL OR OF THE INFINITE

On the hottest day of the last ten summers
a man is sprawled in his backyard hammock
in submission and retreat from concepts
not worrying about eternity or the infinite
unconcerned with anything larger
than the beads of sweat on his body
reminders of the natural order of things
cause and effect, here and there,
what goes up, must ...
then he sees a tiny spider
on his big toe
perched there like a recalcitrant enemy
poisonous, the word *poisonous*, intrudes,
poisonous like a black widow spider,
it is a black widow spider, he thinks
not that he knows the ways
of such creatures
a tarantula he could recognize in an instant
and amidst his spidery thoughts
the recalcitrant enemy
starts its slow and methodical journey
up his leg
too terrified to move
to upset the venomous enemy
he freezes with fear
on the hottest day of the last ten summers
and before the spider
reaches his heart
his heart gives out
and his last thought
is not of the eternal or of the infinite
but the word *poisonous*.
A day latter a young girl
a budding spider collector
finds the tiny creature
and lets it crawl onto her arm
and marvels at God's delicate creation
and tells the tiny creature,
"You are my friend
my very best friend."

First published in Misshapenness (Ekstasis Editions, 2009).

Carl 'Papa' Palmer
UNIVERSITY PLACE, WASHINGTON

Carl 'Papa' Palmer is retired from the military and Federal Aviation Administration (FAA), and is now enjoying life as 'Papa' to his grand descendants, and being a Franciscan Hospice volunteer. His motto is: *"Long Weekends Forever!"*
E: carlpalmer@hotmail.com

HIS LIMBO SOLILOQUY

Actually, I like lockdown. I already was before COVID anyway,
but now I've got my privacy. No family feeling forced to visit
or hold vigil in my netherworld, he confides through the phone.

Both of us former Army soldiers placing us on common ground
made introductions easier with the usual "where were we when"
comparisons of duty assignments all military members embrace.

Though sharing multiple telephone calls these past seven months
since my assignment to be his companion as a hospice volunteer,
I have yet to meet him face-to-face due to pandemic restrictions.

Using his bedside number at the nursing home I can call anytime,
not worry about visiting hours, ask if he's busy, got time to talk.

His answer's most always the same, *Just busy here being alone,*
too close to death to complain. Clicking me to speaker he begins
what he calls "me-memories from a time when when was when."

Mostly musing of being anywhere but there, lost in an actual place,
blurring "what was with what is" behind and in front of his shadow,
recalling dreams as a younger man, of a future in past perfect tense.

And times talking of present times from his no man's land outpost,
All days end as they begin in purgatory, today recopying yesterday,
cared for by hosts of faceless masked angels not letting me die alone.

Forgive me only thinking of myself, I just need you to hear I'm here.
Inside I'm your age, the two of us sharing a brew at the NCO club,
years ago and oceans away, comrades-in-arms talking of our day.

To me he's the sergeant with permanent change of station orders
in transition for his final mission, ending his time on active service,
in hopes his God is religious and his terminal assignment is good.

Pamela Brothers Denyes
VIRGINIA BEACH, VIRGINIA

Pamela's career-based writing included contracted non-fiction, instructional design and manuals, developmental and copy editing, and online/print writing for her regional newspaper and internet gateway. Pamela's poems are published in the *Virginia Bards Central Review, Poetry Society of Virginia Journal* and the *Virginia Writers Club Journal*. Her work is also featured in *Wingless Dreamer's A Tribute to Lord Byron* and her chapbook, *Renewal: Cultivating My Better Self,* received an Honourable Mention in a 2020 National Poetry Writing Month Contest. Pamela's poems have also won or placed in other contests. Now retired, she's harvesting 40 years of poetry, journals and travelogues to create new works - and fun!
E: pamelabrothersdenyes@gmail.com

HAND-WRITTEN NOTE

A friend sent a hand-made card, with a
hand-written note, with the new stamp
commemorating my favourite garden.
Social distancing beautifully accomplished.

I miss our walks with lunch, delicious
speciality desserts split for two spoons.
Her husband has a life-altering disease,
which has also altered their relationship.

Several times I've thought she was ready
to watch him leave as he says he wants to,
to go to Texas to die near his only son.
She's okay with that and so am I.

But he's still with her, here in Virginia,
where we're all on pandemic alert,
staying put until it's safe to travel again.
She did not mention him in her note.

Gayle Bell
DALLAS, TEXAS

Gayle identifies as a LGBTQY woman with a disability, her work has been featured in poetry and art venues across the state, and her poetry has been published in a large number of anthologies, print and online publications. In 2018 she performed *Black Betty, That Thangs Gone Wild*, with Cara Mia's Storytellers, Building Communities. In 2013-2014, she was a co-docent for *My Immovable Truth-A Dallas Lineage*. She facilitated her and other GLBTQY's oral history and performances, sponsored by (MAP-Make Art With Purpose) and displayed at the African American Museum in Dallas.
E: taurusdagger@gmail.com

THREE GIRL ROPE

Rita, Martha, & Me
2 holds the rope
one jumps the rope
banded together
past cooties, breasts, boys
hot foot
slap on asphalt heat
slide past the days

Rita freckles cute baby face
Hi-sidin and smiling
Sand lot wars now forgotten
I think she's in the medical profession

Martha
Nice, quiet fellow poet
Rhyming chiming words, made postcards for me
ran away not too long after I did
Went to Cali, became a musician

Me
Cat eyeglasses and out-dated clothes
Books were my anchor, a thinly held madness
Rita, and Martha, the only sane parts of my life
When all around me blew

Rita, Martha & Me
2 holds the rope
one jumps the rope
banded past cooties, breasts, boys

Mark Tarallo

WASHINGTON DC

Mark is an American writer and journalist. His poetry has appeared in a large number of publications including *Abbey, Beltway Poetry Journal, Innisfree Poetry Journal, Manorborn*, and *Vine Leaves Literary Journal*, as well as the anthologies *District Lines, Insulatus, The Best of Vine Leaves Literary Journal 2012, Surprised by Joy, A Celebration of Winter,* and *Quintessence: Aspects of the Soul*. His awards include the Washington Writing Prize for poetry, and a first-place award in the Virginia Poetry Contest. He is a two-time winner of the Arlington Moving Words (poem-on-a-bus) Poetry Competition.
E: taral566@yahoo.com
W: www.goodreads.com/author/show/6537634.Mark_Tarallo
FB: @mark.tarallo.9

ULYSSES OF THE BARS

Those night rides along the towpath
with Chanticleer and Q, silver flasks
clinking on belt buckles, gravel shushing
under tires like the sound of distant waves.
The air velvet, the sky ecstatic with stars.

Stopping for a few sips on the canal,
lungs heaving with great draughts
of cool rapture. Gentleman, you'd say
our purpose holds to sail beyond the sunset,
far beyond our desks. I stand here
as a man of substance - so let me
ease your journey and you packed the pipe
with the same hand

that once rested on Licia's shoulder
as you teetered around that party,
never losing the tourist's pleasure in the
lush and blurry landscape of your drunkenness.
Your breath nearly set my ear aflame as you
bent close to whisper
I am just so crushed right now, T-man,
Just so so crushed …

At your wedding, ten, maybe twenty nods of recognition
At the groping words of your best man:
The thing about Whit is, there's something heroic about him
Then the limo whisked away you and J
and I was left to party down with your boys.

Through the haze, I could feel again
that scorching weekday noon: humid beyond redemption,
sidewalks brutalized under purposeful strides, the city
set to sink under its own banality.
I saw you break free from a sea of monkey suits
On the corner of Connecticut and K

and sprint madly across the street as the light turned -
knees pumping high, tie blown back like a rudder.
Your body mocked the approaching cars; it seemed so vigorous
I imagined it emitting concentric waves of energy
that would sweep through all of downtown, changing

the rhythm of the streets from a sad Sousa death march
to a delirious Fats Waller swing.
There were several what-an-idiot scowls, but
no matter: they knew not your powers, how you ennobled
the following of sport, how you made the language new.

These days, the lawn needs mowing in Ithaca.
When the world and the boss are both
on your case, you go walk the dog
and sneak a few hits. Sometimes, alone in a bar, I wonder
what you would have said, back then, to the woman

three stools down. Well hail fire, I'm just a farmer
from Poolesville. You one of them naughty city girls?
Then switch from goof to geek
with a few Buck Mulligan riffs, maybe his blasphemous ballad,
and although you'd get shut down, vengeance would later be ours
as we'd toast her blank stare in the face of your allusions.

But now I stare, at my in-box, waiting
for what never arrives.
The stars are shining, T-man.
Q and Chanticleer are filling their flasks as we speak.
Tis not too late to seek a newer world.
Care to join in the cuddle?

John Johnson
MCLEAN, VIRGINIA

John is a poet and entrepreneur. His prior work has been published in *Sundial Magazine, The Boston Literary Magazine, What Rough Beast*, *The Metaworker* and *Unique Poetry*.
E: jjohnson@edgewortheconomics.com
W: www.PoemsOverCoffee.com

THE MAN OF STEEL

A trainer at a snooty gym,
But he wasn't like the others.
Yes, he had the body of a Greek God.
But it became apparent very soon
His strongest muscle was his heart.

And so my training commenced
Begrudgingly showing up at my overpriced gym,
Inferiority complex in full swing
6:30 AM my extra grumpy time
Inconsistently showing up for months,
Hiding from him, and myself.

But somewhere on our journey,
A bond began to form.

For this man was far more than a trainer.
Zenmaster.
Cheerleader.
Counsellor.
Protector.
My biggest fan.

For what he actually taught me all these years.
Had nothing to do with weights and fitness,
But the value of true friendship.

He is a man of steel.
The strongest man I know.
Not just his biceps.
But his heart.
An unbreakable bond between us...
My bicep brother for life.

Chad Norman
CANADA

Chad lives beside the high-tides of the Bay of Fundy, Truro, Nova Scotia. He has given talks and readings in Denmark, Sweden, Wales, Ireland, Scotland, America, and across Canada. His poems appear in publications around the world, and have been translated into Danish, Albanian, Romanian, Turkish, Italian, Spanish, Chinese, and Polish. His collections are *Selected & New Poems* (Mosaic Press), and *Squall: Poems In The Voice Of Mary Shelley* (Guernica Editions). *Simona: A Celebration of the S.P.C.A.* will be out early 2021 (Cyberwit.Net). E: namronskichacha@gmail.com

NOTICE: PARENTS TO BE
In Memory Of Mick Burrs (1940-2021)

The fierce eye of a female robin
fixed on her famous eggs
the nest I believed was abandoned.

Sometimes I long for fur
but lately it is feathers I wish
covered the body I live within.

What it must feel like
to have under you the young
the heat of your body will
bring to that crucial moment,
beak through the egg's shell.

Out where the air also contains
my hope, which is
made up of a wish,
no crow or bluejay is hungry
enough to steal what she
and her mate, keeping guard
in the woken budding oak,
deserve to feed
and fly south together soon.

RANDOM STANZAS IN MEMORY OF HEATHER SPEARS (1935-2021)

I wish
to take
your face in the
trusty fingers my hands
have to offer,
all the wish
wants to be.

I sit
on a
stone waiting in a hope
as sturdy as it is
with a second wish,
to see the chipmunk
April-chill brought close
during another
Nova Scotian Spring.

I think
of Yevtushenko's I,
how he
stood alone in a country
when 1950s Russia
had the poets we now read,
when we take advantage
of his available words.

I walk
out into the mellow year
even though a virus
rules us
regardless of hair left uncut,
and certain arses
left unkicked
there in the house
occupied by liars
who worship white skin.

I cry
knowing not what to do
with the news

of you and your 86 years
leaving us,
only to feel the hugs
shared there in Copenhagen,
shared in the sun
finding the windows
of your thankful gallery.

Anne Mitchell
CARMEL, CALIFORNIA

For Anne the year 2020 gifted her solitude, a chance to slow down, observe and focus on her poetry. A year of Wild Writing Circles have been both anchor and flame for thoughts to flourish and become poems. Anne's recent work may be found in the *Community Journal* for writers.
E: annemitchell9@icloud.com

CROSSING THE BONNEVILLE SALT FLATS WITH GNAT

Dedicated to my daughter Maeve, who is my best travelling buddy ...

We left Salt Lake City at dawn, westward
on I-80, onyx river over salt,
daughter furled in a seat-belted nest,

my co-pilot lost in deep space sleep
as the white flats engulf us into a mirage
of morning, a Volvo asteroid on trajectory

over landscapes of Pluto, wrapped
in a sawtooth horizon, a lake of milk -
I am tempted to wake her, "check out this scene!

tough ride in wagons for the Donner party."
Cue the fill-in first mate, innocent nervy
Gnat, stowaway or shanghaied hitch-hiker,

I do not try to catch him, but welcome enthusiastic
aerials In my sightline over the dash, for he's my new friend,
my partner now- we're explorers at the aurora

hour of rose. "Gnat! did you see that?" he backflips
as we spot the tower, a bouquet of planets,
a behemoth cactus blossoms, spinning

arcs of the cosmos sculpted in turquoise,
lemon and ruby mosaic. A figure eight of glee
from Gnat as the roadside art show unfolds-green tires

of a sea serpent then tail, fin and incisors of a shark,
a baby doll in burlap kneels at Stonehenge in bottles.
When the lake ends, a rest stop at the edge,

I unlatch the door, and Gnat is sucked
out, "Gnat, no!" my daughter awakes and asks,
"who are you talking to?"

Zev Torres
NEW YORK CITY

Zev is a writer and spoken word performer whose work contains elements of both the surreal and real, and draws on the interchange between the volitional and the reflexive. Zev's poetry has appeared in numerous print and on-line publications including *Great Weather for Media's I Let Go of the Stars in my Hand*, *Escape Wheel* and *Suitcase of Chrysanthemums,* Three Rooms Press' *Journal of Contemporary Dada Writing and Art, Maintenant 6* and *Maintenant 12,* several Brownstone Poets' anthologies, *Verses of Silence, Athena Review, Breadcrumbs, Nerve Lantern,* Mad Gleam Press' *PostStranger, The Wild Word, Literary Orphan* and *Ty(po-e:tic)us*. Zev has featured at many New York City spoken word venues and, since 2008, has hosted Make Music New York's annual Spoken Word Extravaganza. In 2010, Zev founded the Skewered Syntax Poetry Crawls.
E: zevtorres@hotmail.com

LIKE ALWAYS

You could have told me, you know.
I don't know why you didn't.
I wouldn't have judged you because,
That's not what friends do.
So, I don't understand why you didn't tell me,
Because I'm your closest friend and
We've always told each other everything
And being friends means
Never keeping secrets from each other, right?
Because that's not what friends do,
And friends don't judge each other, just like
I'm not judging you now and never would,
And you know that but, still, you didn't tell me,
Like maybe you thought I would judge you, and
I don't understand why because you know I wouldn't
So that doesn't make any sense to me and
I ended up finding out online when you posted about it,
Found out the same way everyone else found out about it
Even though I'm not everyone else,
But I would have been there for you
While you were going through it,
And wouldn't have judged you,
And could have shown you support and all that
Which I'm sure you could have used,
But for some reason you didn't let me, but
That's okay, I'm not angry, maybe a little surprised,
But I'm sure you had your reasons so,
Whenever you want to talk that'll be okay,
And you don't have to apologize because
Being friends means never having to apologize
Even if you've done something stupid.
So, whenever you want to talk,
I'm here for you,
Like always.
I'm here.
Whenever you want to to talk.

OH WELL

Is it time to inhale or exhale?
It is easy —
For me at least —
To lose the rhythm
When those late afternoon alerts arrive:
"Dad is in the hospital";
"Headline: The entire world is suffering delirium tremens";
"How's the writing going?"

Could have answered rhetorically,
Said something like: "welcome back"
And left it at that,
Or simply asked what this was about —
Another opportunity to play whack-a-dream?
Instead of wasting my time
Sorting through old song titles,
Looking for one that captured,
To my satisfaction,
The sensation.
Oh well.

Fortunately we had the good sense
Not to exceed our allotment of words.
Or to resort to off-the-rack sentiment.
That much we have in common.

In other respects we are oppositional,
The way most everyone else is.
Your preference is to reside out of sight,
Unnoticed,
Reclining in doubt.
My tendency is to trip up the stairs,
To lose my footing after the ice has melted,
And the sidewalks are dry,

To manage more gracefully the chaos,
Than the preceding or ensuing tranquillity,
While peeling the skin off of my beliefs,
Seeking their core

Stay in touch. Or not.
Either way you will continue to vex me

With the turmoil you instigate,
Intentionally or not;
With that fleck of pulsing light you imbedded
In a cloud that never drifts completely out of view;
With those trip wires strung around
The permanent encampment you maintain
In my all-too-vulnerable imagination.

Marie C. Lecrivain
LOS ANGELES, CALIFORNIA

Marie is a poet, publisher, and ordained priestess in the Ecclesia Gnostica Catholica - the ecclesiastical arm of Ordo Templi Orientis. She's lived and thrived in Los Angeles for the last 27 years. Her work has been published in *California Quarterly, Gargoyle, Nonbinary Review, Orbis, Pirene's Fountain*, and many other journals. She's the author of several books of poetry and fiction, and recent editor of *Gondal Heights: A Bronte Tribute Anthology*.
E: mariel671@gmail.com
FB: @marieclecrivainauthor

CARYN P

Some days, I see you waving at me from the fork in the road where we parted on good terms. My 11-year-old self took no notice of the signs; the sudden pink flush in your cheeks, the eagerness in your voice, and the way your eyes scanned the sky, as if your wings were already unfurled to bear you aloft on celestial winds. I didn't know you were saying farewell, that Death, in a brief moment of whimsy, lent you a glamour that fooled us all, so used to seeing you, pale and slow-moving, puffy from chemo and inactivity, struggle against the intruder that stole your childhood. You were already gone, even as we embraced, and promised to see each other again. It was your departure, announced that following Sunday, at mass, that taught three things: always question what I see, I'll miss you forever, and this is the most brutal way to birth a poet.

Linda Imbler
WICHITA, KANSAS

Linda's published paperback poetry collections include *Big Questions, Little Sleep, Big Questions, Little Sleep: Second Edition, Lost and Found, Red Is The Sunrise,* and *Bus Lights, Travel Sights: Nashville and Back.* She has three e-books published by Soma Publishing; *The Sea's Secret Song, Pairings* - which is a hybrid e-book of short fiction and poetry - and *That Fifth Element.* Her fourth e-book entitled *Per Quindecim* will be published by Soma Publishing in 2021. Linda has been nominated for a Pushcart Prize, and has four Best Of The Net nominations. When not writing, Linda is an avid reader, classical guitar player, and a practitioner of both Yoga and Tai Chi, and helps her husband, a Luthier, build acoustic guitars.
E: mike-imbler@cox.net
W: www.lindaspoetryblog.blogspot.com

JAN

I had a friend who believed in Heaven.
A smart lady, who spoke with God.
She knew she was being heard.
Here, she had many abilities
and she was brave and feared little.

She had dabbled in magick,
lighting candles of different colours
and chanting over their flames
to bring about specific effects.
I never understood this behaviour,
in parallel to her church-going ways.

She claimed that God's church
and the Kiowa teachings of her youth
and the Wiccan creeds were not at odds.
She said anything done on behalf of another,
if done with love, could not be a wrong thing.

We watched the sunsets in Key West
for several evenings in a row
while vacationing there.
She told me of her faiths
and her lack of fear about dying,
although at the time she did not know
that within a few years, that would be her reality.

I told her while she was ill
that she was facing it so bravely.
She smiled, as that seemed to please her.
I was not there for her last breaths,
but I suspect she literally heard God guiding her that night.

I know she was speaking to him.

Wil Michael Wrenn
CHARLESTON, MASSACHUSETTS

Wil is a poet, songwriter, and musician. He has an MFA from Lindenwood University, and is a songwriter/publisher member of ASCAP (American Society of Composers, Authors, and Publishers). He has had individual poems published in many journals and several anthologies, and has published three books of poems; *Songs of Solitude, Seasons of a Sojourner, Enid Lake Mosaic*, the latter two having been published by Silver Bow Publishing.
E: CelticPoet@gmx.com
W: www.michaelwrenn.webstarts.com

I'LL REMEMBER YOU

You touched me, moved me,
changed me forever,
simply by being who you are.
Please remember me;
I'll surely remember you.
Every time I see a baby smile,
or a Christmas tree,
or falling snow,
I'll remember you.
Every time I hear
the laughter of a child,
I'll remember you.
Every time I see an autumn sky,
I'll remember your eyes.
Every time I hear
the wind whisper softly
in the evening mist,
I'll remember your voice.
I'll remember you
every time I see something beautiful,
gentle and good,
honest and true.
I hope you'll remember me;
please remember me
because I'll surely remember you -
always.

Russell Willis
ESSEX JUNCTION, VERMONT

Ethicist and online education entrepreneur, Russell emerged as a poet in 2019. Since then, his poetry has been published (or accepted for publication) in *Intangible Magazine, 433, Breathe, Peeking Cat, Le Merle, As Above So Below, Grand Little Things, Frost Meadow Review's Pandemic Poetry, October Hill, Cathexis Northwest, Meat for Tea, The MOON magazine, Snapdragon: A Journal of Art & Healing, Tiny Seed Literary Journal, The Esthetic Apostle*, and three anthologies. Russell grew up in and around Texas, was vocationally scattered throughout the Southwest and Great Plains for many years, and is now settled in Essex Junction with his wife, Dawn.
E: willisdrr63@gmail.com
W: www.REWillisWrites.com

KNOWN

The gift of being known
Not merely acknowledged
Known
Reciprocated by being knowable
Open, vulnerable, deeply vulnerable, perfectly vulnerable
In a world that knows no perfection
Trusting that the original gift
Was an act of trustworthiness
Accepting the trustworthiness
Unconditionally
Itself a gift
That comfort in being known
That satisfaction
That strength
Untethered yet thoroughly connected
The condition necessary for unconditional love
To be offered

Rich Orloff
NEW YORK CITY

Although fairly new at writing poetry, Rich has been writing plays for decades. The *New York Times* called his play *Big Boys* "rip-roaringly funny," and named *Funny As A Crutch* a Critic's Pick. During the year until the pandemic struck, he travelled the USA performing his one-person show *It's A Beautiful Wound*. Last spring his documentary-style play *Days Of Possibilities* had eight productions (over Zoom) to commemorate the 50th anniversary of the killings at Kent State University. His short plays have had over 2000 productions. During late 2020 and the first half of 2021, he shaped 60 poems he wrote into the theatre piece, *Blessings From The Pandemic*, which had over a dozen presentations (mostly over Zoom) by theatres, schools, churches and synagogues across the United States, and which was chosen as one of the first plays to be licensed by Theatrical Rights Worldwide.

E: richplays@gmail.com
W: www.richorloff.com
W: www.trwplays.com

ALICE

The sun is setting on a friend I haven't seen in over a year
It's only dusk
But I can tell darkness is approaching
The words are simpler
The feelings flutter about like butterflies
The moment is all
A second ago is a distant memory

She's had a full life
Three husbands, and several more lovers
Two careers
A child and a grandchild
Poverty and wealth
Letting go of some kinds of happiness to hold onto others

She's furious that she needs a health aide
And grateful for her presence
She's furious at how closely her daughter watches over her
And is overjoyed at how closely her daughter watches over her

It's been quite a day
She has had trouble understanding my words
A problem with her new hearing aid, she says
A moment later
She marvels at the chirp of a bird
As the sun sets just a little more

LindaAnn LoSchiavo
NEW YORK CITY

LindaAnn is a dramatist, writer, and poet. Her poetry collections *Conflicted Excitement* (Red Wolf Editions, 2018), *Concupiscent Consumption* (Red Ferret Press, 2020), and Elgin Award nominee *A Route Obscure and Lonely* (Wapshott Press, 2020) along with her collaborative book on prejudice (Macmillan in the USA, Aracne Editions in Italy) are her latest titles. A member of The Dramatists Guild and SFPA, she was recently Poetry Superhighway's 'Poet of the Week.'
Twitter: @Mae_Westside

IMPATIENS BUDDING

What keeps us up? Your friendship's all I have —
Riches I couldn't be extravagant
With, spiritual broth concocted, stirred
Long years ago, left undiluted. I'd
Be running, empty; your blue eyes refuelled
Me through the peace of simply being there.

Between us, even harmless quirks absorbed
Raw energy and meaning, buoyed us up.

What's happening today? Our picnic rained
Us in. Your blanket on the floor, we faced
Glass garden doors. Through passion of the storm,
I saw a plant I'd given you that time
You struggled with a fever, lay bed-bound.

It's grown — that red impatiens balsamina,
Nicknamed the "Touch-Me-Not" — forgotten now
And pelted by surprising downfalls. "I'll
Go rescue it!" I say, aware you've just
Been eyeing up my legs, inclined towards me
In all new ways. I don't know what to say.

Am I imagining this? Underneath
My naked legs, this fabric touches off
Unnameable anxieties of you
In bed too ill to do the simple things
That I dropped by to do for helpless you,
Two trapped by passion of uncertainty
Back then — perhaps again fond victims touched,
Arresting fever, guarded, wondering
As tight impatiens buds are poised for first
Direction, naturally inclined (though still
Unseeing) towards heat's light. That storm keeps up.

New buds stay down. For you, old friend, I hold
Aloft the peace of all I won't deny.

> Today we're watchful apple pickers rained
> Out of the garden. Not for us. Not yet.

Lou Faber
PORT ST. LUCIE, FLORIDA

Lou's work has previously appeared in *Atlanta Review, Arena Magazine, Exquisite Corpse, Rattle, Eureka Literary Magazine, Borderlands:* the *Texas Poetry Review, Midnight Mind, Pearl, Midstream, European Judaism, Greens Magazine, The Amethyst Review, Afterthoughts, The South Carolina Review* and *Worcester Review*, and in small journals in India, Pakistan, China and Japan, among many others. Lou has also been nominated for a Pushcart Prize.
E: lfaberfl@outlook.com
W: www.anoldwriter.com
W: www.bird-of-the-day.com

MY ANNA

Along the banks of the barge canal
in the village park, a man
older, his hair white, almost
a mane, sits on the breakwall
feeding Wonder bread
to the small flotilla of ducks.
Tearing shreds of crust
from a slice, he casts it
onto the water and smiles
as they bob for the crumbs.
He tells them the story
of his life as though
there were oldest friends.
My Anna, he says,
was a special woman,
I met her one night
in the cramped vestibule
of an Indian take away
in London during a blackout.
We heard the sirens and then
a blast, not far off.
She grabbed my arm in fear.
She was from Marlow on Thames
she lived in a small flat
in the Bottom, she worked
days in a millinery,
and at night tended bar
at the Local, until the war.
She's been gone two years now
and I miss her terribly
especially late at night.
A goose slowly swims over
awaiting her meal, she
looks deeply into his eyes.
How are you, dearest Anna,
it is not the same without you
late at night when the silence
is broken again by the sirens.

SHARED VISION, ONCE REMOVED

Stevie and I were probably eight
sitting on the front stoop of our flat
he the only one third grade smaller than me.
There was no snow to be seen,
none in the sky, none on the frozen
and still patchy lawn, just the wind
of an always cold December day.
Christmas is coming, I said
aren't you excited, with all the gifts.
Stevie smiled, they're always great
but maybe this year I'll finally meet Santa.
I laughed, lacking the heart
to shatter an infantile dream.
Do you buy into the sled
and reindeer thing, or does he come
more by way of magic.
Of course it's the sled, but
I wouldn't be surprised
if it had some pretty good jet engines.
And you think he comes
down the chimney I asked.
We don't have one, you know that
so he must use a back window,
the one where I broke the lock
last summer when we were spies.
He looked momentarily sad,
you don't have anything like Santa,
although you get lots of neat gifts,
just not all at once.
At least eight, most years more
but you're right we have no Santa,
but we have something even better.
Better how, what could be better?
Each year at Passover, Elijah
comes in during our Seder
I don't see him but we have
to open the door for him during dinner.
Does he bring you anything?
He's not like that, he just comes
all old and bearded, and
before you can even see him
he's gone again, probably next door

at the Goldstein's or maybe
with Larry Finkel, though his mom
can't cook very well.
So what's he do, this Elijah?
Not much, I admitted,
but he does have a drinking problem.

Donna Zephrine
NEW YORK CITY

Donna was born in Harlem, New York and grew up in Bay Shore, Long island. She graduated from Columbia University School of Social Work in May 2017, and currently works for the New York State Office of Mental Health at Pilgrim Psychiatric Center Outpatient SOCR (State Operated Community Residence). She is a combat veteran who completed two tours in Iraq. She was on active duty army, stationed at Hunter Army Airfield 3rd infantry Division as a mechanic. Since returning home, Donna enjoys sharing her experiences and storytelling through writing. Donna's stories most recently have been published in *New York Times, On The Road, War and Battle, The Seasons, Qutub Minar Review, Bards Initiative, Radvocate, Oberon, Long Island Poetry Association* and *The Mighty*.

E: kauldonna@yahoo.com
FB: @donna.zephrine
Twitter: @dzephrine
Instagram: @donnazephrine
LinkenIn: @donna-zephrine-30300636

AN ANGEL IN A BOOKSTORE
For Pastor Larry Mancini

I met Pastor Mancini at the Barnes and Noble book store,
I was studying for the state boards in social work.
He was conducting a bible study workshop
The group usually sat at the round table adjacent to me.
I overheard them talking about scriptures in the bible.
As I was passing someone in the group said hello.
We spoke a little bit and they invited to join
I met with the bible group a few times
Paster Mancini helped me renew my faith
I added him as a friend on Facebook messenger
He helped me understand that
god is in control and knows and sees and will lead me
In the right direction.
He was there to counsel and pray with me when I needed someone to
talk to.
I feel having a spiritual friend, mentor and advisor is important.
When I am sad or depressed he is a person I could turn to
for help in turning a negative situation to a positive outlook.
Thank you Pastor Larry Mancini

Joan Leotta

CALABASH, NORTH CAROLINA

Joan plays with words on page and stage. Her poems, essays, and articles have been published - or are forthcoming - in *Visual Verse, Pure Slush, Verse Virtual, Writing in a Woman's Voice, Pine Song, The Ekphrastic Review, Potato Soup, Eastern Iowa Review, Mystery Tribune*, and others. She's been a Tupelo 30/30 writer and Gilbert Chappell Fellow. Her chapbook *Languid Lusciousness with Lemon* is out from Finishing Line Press. Other poetry works available are: *Nature's Gifts* (Stanzaic Stylings), *Dancing Under the Moo*n and *Morning by Morning*, mini-chapbooks published with Origami Press. She performs personal and folk tales featuring food, family, and strong women. When she is not at computer or in front of a crowd, she roams local beaches in search of seabirds to photograph and seashells to collect.
E: joanleotta@gmail.com

WHERE DID MY BELOVED FRIEND, GO?

My beloved red-tailed hawk,
friend and fierce inspiration, daily
watched over me as I drove by
his hunting ground.
Magnificent in his aerie on the
telephone wires, as he waited
for the occasional vole or mouse
to skitter by, he would nod
that noble head at me.
Now and then, for a few days
he would shift to another place,
then return to greet me from
his highwire perch on my drive.

My neighbour who keeps hens,
sells chicks and eggs.
Two months ago, a sign
announced chicks were born
in that round, fenced chicken coop.
Dawn, when ducks and deer
feed and are fed upon,
shotgun blasts often puncture
early morning quiet.
However, I have begun to fret,
my dear friend, was perhaps seen
swooping down on my neighbour's chicks.
I sometimes fear one blast
may have caught him, although
more often my heart tells me
he escaped, soaring high,
circling, but then deserting
this precinct for another.
I still look for him as I drive by
his favourite perch. My hope
for his return ebbs as summer
moves into fall; my heart
imagines him hunting happily
in his new locale, perhaps
also missing me.

The neighbour's sign still advertises eggs,
but I will never stop to buy them.

FRIENDSHIP

Sit next to me in school,
on the bus.
Play with me at recess.
Loan your hankie to dry my tears.
Laugh with me when I fall;
cheer me when I rise.
I will do the same for you.

STRAWBERRIES

Strawberries —
Cherokee love fruit.
Tossed in the path
of an angry wife
racing away after
her husband
disappointed her,
worked their magic when
seeing their
ruby red beauty,
she tasted one and its
sweetness charmed
her. Anger melted.

I think on this as I slice
these heart shaped treats
for my dearest and myself.
We argued this morning.
I pick up a slice, eat it
then walk into the living
room to give him a kiss.
Friendship in marriage
is the sweetest fruit.

John Laue
LA SELVA BEACH, CALIFORNIA

John is a teacher/counsellor, and a former editor of *Transfer, San Francisco Review* and *Monterey Poetry Review.* He has won awards for his writing including the Ina Coolbrith Poetry Prize at The University of California, Berkeley. With five published poetry books, the last *A Confluence of Voices Revisited* (Futurecycle Press), and a book of prose advice for people with psychiatric diagnoses (*The Columns of Joel Mobius*), he presently coordinates the reading series of The Monterey Bay Poetry Consortium.
E: Joelmobius@aol.com

FIREWORKS (AND MAD TOGETHER)

You must change your life Rilke

It was at Rich's cheap apartment complex,
a honeycomb in the congested city,
the argument upstairs, the scream,
the heavy footsteps scraping, stumbling,
then the final thump
so hard our ceiling light blinked out,
and afterward, the sirens,
fire truck, ambulance, police.

They carried her out on a stretcher.
The man followed in his car.
Rich volunteered they'd seemed
a loving couple. But this!
He couldn't believe it.

I knew better, had seen it before
with my father and stepmother,
her the aggressor, not him.
And afterward, when he awoke
from the force of her blow,
her promise not to do it again.
But the rage remained
and we learned how to duck.

So I thought I knew this man.
therapy? It might help.
But who would pay?
Jail? She'd withdraw the charges,
be content with promises
not to hit, to hurt, to maim.
The world said Rich was crazy,
the couple sane. But
with him the same husband,
her the same wife,
what each of them needed
was a different life!

Janet McCann
COLLEGE STATION, TEXAS

Janet work has been published in a large number of publications including *Kansas Quarterly, Parnassus, Nimrod, Sou'wester, America, Christian Century, Christianity and Literature, New York Quarterly, Tendri*l, and others. A 1989 NEA Creative Writing Fellowship winner, she taught At Texas A & M University from 1969 until 2015, is now Professor Emerita. she has co-edited anthologies with David Craig, *Odd Angles of Heaven* (Shaw, 1994), *Place of Passage* (story line, 2000), and *Poems of Francis And Clare* (St. Anthony Messenger, 2004). she has written three poetry books and six chapbooks. Her most recent poetry book: *The Crone at The Casino* (Lamar University Press, 2014). She also has co-authored two textbooks, and written a book on Wallace Stevens titled: *Wallace Stevens: The Celestial Possible* (Twayne, 1996).
E: j-mccann1@tamu.edu

ELEGY FOR LEE
In Memory of Lee Nicholson

You were so polite, embarrassed
When I bumped into you wearing a towel
At the summer seminar residence.

You loved old things, and gave me once
A print of a mythical animal; in the print
(1700s I think) he was quite real.

Our friendship had no ordinary context.
I never met your people nor did you
Mine, though we explored our pasts

Half the night after sessions. You had been
A child evangelist and that had marked you.
Your poetry was delicately beautiful

And yet daring. You calligraphed it,
Sent me "Dante's Cat" and "Lady Nike,"
Words swirled into images; now they hang

In corners of my office. You would not publish
Though many would have loved your work.
In the dungeon of Princeton's library

We ate machine snacks and talked God,
Greek myth and poetry. Every Christmas after,
Long letters and poems crossed in the mail

Until this year's came back. Alarmed, I searched;
You'd gone. Of course no one would tell me;
We existed only in those passing words.

The exquisite distinction of your friendship
Gone like a butterfly in its migration;
I'm hoping it has landed somewhere green.

OLD FRIEND

Around your eyes the flesh crinkles
as your ancient car flies by the past.
New structures, old ones gone
though street names remain.

My eyes more blurred, more moist.
Your hands have knobs, mine spots.
How many dogs ago were we here?
Now: the bad neighbours gone

and the new man there now mowing,
his eyebrows a question. Next door,
the crumbling crack house sold
to a young couple, both up on the roof

with tar and shingles. Where we were
gone now. The way you were,
to act, to take the lead
decisive with compassion, still there.

Jill Sharon Kimmelman
DELAWARE

Jill is a Pushcart Prize nominee. Her international publication credits include *Vita Brevis Press, Spillwords Press, Fine Lines Journal, Loveoffood.net, Poetic Musings Ezine, HeartBeats, an Anthology* (2021)*, Scentsibility, an Anthology*, (2020), *Two Hearts, ILA Literary Magazine, Stab The Pomegranate* and multiple poetry videos from Sparrow Productions. Her first book *You Are The Poem*, a coffee table collection of poems and photos in b&w and colour, by Jill and her husband - a former professional photographer - is scheduled for release in November, 2021.
E: jskimmelman@icloud.com

TRADING WISHES

It was winter
the only posies to be found had been forced
into bloom in some distant hothouse
that turned them into hybrids and stole their
scent away

I wrote you a letter proposing
a porch swing to share and
hours upon hours of unhurried conversation

Do you remember?

Finally spring has arrived
the flowers on my bedside table are luscious
sun-drenched yellow tulips
and the streets beneath my windows are ablaze
with magnificent blossoms

As far back as I remember...once I had my
longed-for-license-to-drive-in-one-hand and
the keys-to-my-very-own-sleek-automobile
in the other
I would celebrate spring's arrival with a long drive to
in particular
cruising with the top down and the radio turned up loud

Springtime calls to another lucky girl
my sweet Allegra Belle, behind the wheel of
my candy-apple car
and I believe that the time has come to trade in
"my porch swing wish with you"
for a drive to nowhere in particular
Perhaps a picnic ... a ancient blanket our tablecloth
with a bountiful buffet of yummy things to tickle our tastebuds
fried chicken ... blackberry cobbler ... mangoes so perfectly ripe
that the juice drips down our chins
and endless pitchers of fresh peach Bellinis

You will drive
we will talk of poets and poems ... our favourite books
passions we share despite our separate histories
the blessing and the gift of our precious

"separated-by-only-the-oceans-between-us-friendship
"cooking from the heart"
and how we honour those very special
story-tellers
for they were indeed our earliest muses

Hours will pass unnoticed
whispers of wishes will come to settle in our hearts and minds
and we will scribble the words of
friendship and connection on the canvas of
each other's souls

Though it is but a wish whispered into the wind
I know that you will pick it up
dust it off
and never forget the girl who wished you into it

Though we may never share a porch swing
take that leisurely drive on hidden roads
swig the finest of champagnes
or make angels in the snow
I will forever celebrate the gift of our
enduring friendship

Someday soon
there will be a cloudless azure sky: a reason for joy
and on that glorious spring afternoon
it will indeed be enough

First published in-print and online in *Better Than Starbucks*, (October 2018).

FRIENDS TO THE END

True friends celebrate your victories
believe in your crazy dreams
show up somewhere on your bucket list
love that your heart, like a favourite flower
opens its blossoms to welcome you home
even if it's been quite a while

True friends understand and appreciate the beauty and the blessing
of
of companionable silence
sense when a hug is needed
and when to back away for a little while
embrace the magical healing power of a shared meal
equally delicious conversation
and the gift of a million mixed memories

A true friend is an un-edited poem
who will hold you close
whisper words of comfort and humour
and love you forever
knowing that you, without a moment's hesitation,
will always do the same

Beloved friends, you are priceless gems
to treasure ... cherish ... admire ... trust ... believe in ... and love in
this life
and in all the ones to follow.

First published *Spillwords Press*, (June, 2020)

Debi Schmitz Noriega
DES MOINES, IOWA

Although born and raised in Iowa, Debi spent five years in Denver and nine years in Houston, before returning to her home state to settle with her husband Jaime, two cats and a dog. Debi and her husband have six children and eight grandchildren between them. Debi loves to read, write, collect stamps, design craft books, go to drag racing events with Jaime, and spend as much time as possible surrounded by her family.
E: debi_schmitz@yahoo.com

"SAY, SAY, OH PLAYMATE"

Barbies in swimsuits and high heels,
pen pal letters composed to David Cassidy's fan club,
studying Tiger Beat magazine photos by flashlight in my closet,
estranged from the silly boys of the neighborhood.

Foster Park, one block away,
we'd swing, teeter-totter, and sing,
as we'd run and push the merry-go-round,
only to hop up, hold on, and squeal at the top of our lungs.

Do you remember,
skipping in the damp gutter of leaves and earthworms,
gathering stones for our coveted collections,
and keeping a spongy brown fuzzy ball in a baby food jar
until a million baby spiders crawled out the lid holes my Dad had
punched?

Giggling at "The Pink Panther,"
on cartoon-Saturday mornings,
mimicking the "American Bandstand" dancers,
while sporting our trendy slick vinyl boots.

Sundays, after a lesson from "JOT"
I'd dress for church, white doily on my head.
When back home, I'd switch into play clothes
and rush out the door to find you, in the swing of our apple tree.

Enchanted moments of childhood,
We'd adore my baby sister and imagine our own futures.
Forty-five years later, I wonder if we'd still be best friends,
if only you hadn't moved away.

Susan Zeni
MINNEAPOLIS, MINNESOTA

Susan's work has appeared, among other places, in the *New York Quarterly, The Seattle Weekly*, and the *Minneapolis Star and Tribune* publications in the U.S. cities in which she has lived. She's now living about a mile away from George Floyd Square. Pre-covid, Susan plays accordion in the Polkastra and the Tsatskelehs, as well as solo gigs at art openings, Quaker events, and farmers' markets.
E: susanzeni70@gmail.com

FRIENDS

After sunset, I explore the quartier,
so I won't get lost next morning.
Ladies of the night, rangy as candlesticks,
prop themselves on the ponts de Ile St. Louis,
red laughter and sequins imploding the Seine.
An accordion plays simple in C and G
as I wander out under the sky,
small and alone on the Quai de Bourbon.

Next morning, Brit friends of a poet pal
welcome me in for une petit dejeuner,
"Bonjour amie, bienvenue, bienvenue!"
doors thrown open on the balcony
as clouds twist over the Seine.
Michael's coffee fills the air.
Sylvia, her voice a lovely Jamaican patois,
strokes and smooths her dear friend's hair.
Mascara bleeding, Zoe weeps
after a heartless night on the Pont St Louis,
her spirit a pale pale moth
against the flame of Sylvia's hands
as they brush brush brush the bright orange thatch
as it flutters and fluffs like a wild macaw
as the sun breaks out on the Quai de Bourbon.

Ed Ahern
FAIRFIELD, CONNECTICUT

Ed resumed writing after forty odd years in foreign intelligence and international sales. He's had over three hundred stories and poems published so far, and six books. Ed works the other side of writing at *Bewildering Stories*, where he sits on the review board and manages a posse of six review editors.
E: salmonier@aol.com
FB: @EdAhern73
Instagram: @edwardahern1860
Twitter: @bottomstripper

THE TIME OF DAY

A widow walks by my house each day
in syncopation with the mailman.
She has also lost a daughter,
but what is gone is carried deep,
for she always smiles and stops to chat.
We exchange perhaps two hundred words
about weather and children and neighbours,
but never about the death and absence
so twined into our daily living,
and the knitting we do to cope.
We sense with tacit understanding
that our inanities give unsaid comfort
to our silenced fears and grief.

Alonzo "zO" Gross
BETHLEHEM, PENNSYLVANIA

Alonzo (zO) is a songwriter, dancer, recording artist and writer. His short stories were first published internationally in 2005, and in 2006, in the *Staying Sane* book series published by Evelyn Fazio; *Staying Sane when family comes to visit* (2005) and *Staying Sane during the Thanksgiving Holiday*. His first book of poems entitled *Inspiration, Harmony and the World Within* was published in 2012. Also in that same year he was awarded "Best Spoken Word Poet" at the Lehigh Valley music awards. In 2016, zO was selected as a featured poet in the film "*Voices*" directed by Gina Nemo, filmed in Los Angeles California, and released in 2017 in select theatres, as well as on Amazon Prime. In January of 2018, he released his second book of poetry *sOuL eLiXir The writingZ of zO,* which was greeted with rave reviews. In November 2020, zO was named as one of the best poets of 2020 by Inner Child Press, where his work was featured in their anthology. In June of 2021, zO released his highly anticipates third book of poetry/art *PoemZ 4 U AND Your Z*. zO is a graduate in the field of English Literature from Temple University, and looks forward to releasing music CDs, as well as new books of poetry and art.
E: alonzogross73@gmail.com
FB: @Zo10000angelz
FB:@ Zo-Music-Fan-Page-161339523932691
Instagram: @zoalonzogross

THAT VERY PART OF U ...

He's Touchin' That Very Part of U,
that is cryin' inside -
Clutchin' The Very Part of U,
thas sighin'cause someone lied -.
She's Caressing The Very Part of U,
bruised & ever so battered/
He's Blessing The Very Part of U,
that U choose 2 feel doesn't matter/.
She's Lighting The Very Part of U,
weakened in a state of pain
He's Fighting 4 That Very Part of U,
beatened from The Anguish,
that remains.
She's Praying 4 That Very Part of U,
that thinks She doesn't care
He's Staying,
4 the very thought of Her
makes U breathe "It's Very air".

Lisa Molina
AUSTIN, TEXAS

Lisa has a Bachelor of Fine Arts in Theatre and English Education. While not binging on her new favourite writer's works, she can be found working with students with special needs, writing, singing, playing the piano, or marvelling at nature with her family. Her poetry can be found in several literary journals including *Beyond Words Magazine, Trouvaille Review, Ancient Paths Literary Journal, The Ekphrastic Review, Down in the Dirt, Sad Girls Club Literary Blog, Indolent Books, Silver Birch Poetry and Prose, Amethyst Review*, and soon to be featured in *Peeking Cat*.

E: lisabmolina@gmail.com
W: www.lisalitgeek.wordpress.com
Instagram @lisabookgeek
Twitter @lisabmolina1

RUNNING AWAY

July, 1974

Seeking adventure and fearless freedom,
we decide it's time to run away.

Packing our knapsacks with
Cokes, M&Ms, and pink pyjamas,

we traverse the trail of fairies to the
great green metal cube fortress
with the humming rotating fan
on the side of my house,

and hide behind it,
where

NO
nagging parents,
bratty big brothers, or
annoying little sisters
can find us.

First, we float the purple blanket
onto the sweet smelling
freshly-mowed green grass.

After pulling the tabs off our Cokes,
we clink our cans together in a toast
"To Friendship!"

Proceeding to pop each
red, green, brown, and
yellow M&M into
our mouths, we smile
in the triumph of
our escape.

The afternoon sun scorches on.

And on.

We wonder if anyone will see us

changing out of our shorts and
sweat-covered David Cassidy t-shirts
into our pink pyjamas to sleep
on the purple blanket
behind our fortress.

The west sun
ball of heat
starts to melt our
adventurous spirits,

like the extra M&Ms
melting in our knapsack.

And we remember
that the the fan blade
spinning round and round
on top of the cube-shaped
great green metal fortress,

by some magic,

makes the inside of my house
cool and fresh as a breezy spring
day, when we fly our kites high
in the light blue sky.

And we think of our bedrooms,
with soft plush beds.

And the powder blue bathroom
begins calling to us.

And we start to feel hungry.

Looking in our knapsack,
the extra M&Ms have melted.
The aluminium can sodas now warm.

Sweat
drips
drips
drips
down our backs
in the hot humid
Houston heat of summer ...

"Um, so, I need to go to the bathroom."

"Yeah, it's really hot out here, and the mosquitoes
will be out soon."

"I didn't even think of that!"

Silence.

"You wanna go inside my house? Maybe you could sleep over. And we
can watch Carol Burnet!"

She smiles.

My best friend and I grab
the blanket off the grass
and the knapsack,
walk around the fortress
to my front door.

I open it.
A rush of
cool air hits us,

and we giggle,

knowing that we
ran away
for a day.

Bernadette Perez
BELEN, NEW MEXICO

In 1990 Bernadette received the Silver Poet Award from *World of Poetry*. Published in over 100 publications between 2015 - 2019, her work has appeared in *The Wishing Well; Musings, Small Canyons* anthology*, Poems 4 Peace, Contribution to La Familia: La Casa de Colores, a*nd may others. She was also included in the mega-unity poem by Juan Felipe and *The Americans Museum Inscription* by Shinpei Takeda.
E: bpburritos@aol.com

LEGENDARY DAYS OF CHIVALRY

Young innocence
Joyful memories
Laughter between rainbows
Showers splashing in pouring rain

Thriving dramatic frivolity
Delightful stages
Trickling continuously

A code of conduct
Trueness
Thoughtfulness

Different are the clothes we wear
Layered by rotating differences
Colours alternating
Since my day
Changes

Engage in natural beauty

The moons arrival
A new phase
At peace with natures maturity

Smiles are organic
A facade for criteria
Giggles are music to thy ear
Tiny palms of hands caress air pockets of time
Time that has quickly passed

In cool of wind
Mother calls
With open arms we run to her embrace

Children excited to play
Dreaming of yesterday
Reaping the benefits
Exploring possibilities
Ready for the future

Perhaps above all, play is a simple joy that is a cherished part of
childhood

An unconditional love
Survived by time

An immortal friendship
Based on mutual respect
Connected
Low hanging fruits whom feelings run deep

Soulmates nevertheless
A infinite strong bond
Forged together in perfect harmony

Wilda Morris
BOLINGBROOK, ILLINOIS

Wilda is the Workshop Chair of Poets and Patrons of Chicago, and a past President of the Illinois State Poetry Society. She has published over 700 poems in anthologies, webzines, and print publications, including *The Ocotillo Review, Pangolin Review, Poetry Sky, Whitefish Review, Quill & Parchment* (for which she was the featured poet for November 2020), and *Journal of Modern Poetry*. For three years she chaired the Stevens Poetry Manuscript Competition. She has won awards for formal and free verse and haiku, including the 2019 Founders' Award from the National Federation of State Poetry Societies. Much of the work on her second poetry book, *Pequod Poems: Gamming with Moby-Dick* (published in 2019), was written during a Writer's Residency on Martha's Vineyard. For fifteen years, she has moderated a monthly poetry reading at Brewed Awakening Coffeeshop in Westmont, Illinois. A retired educator, she is working on a book of poetry inspired by books and articles on scientific topics. Her blog features a monthly poetry compertition.
Blog: www.wildamorris.blogspot.com

LAST EVENING IN DOOR COUNTY
For Susan

As night darkens
field and tree line,
we walk a road lit
by an almost full moon.
Doe and robin are nestled in
with their young.

The June breeze
tousles our hair
and hums through
the tops of maple,
pine and birch.

In the distance,
a whippoorwill
trills a lullaby,
while crickets
in the meadow
and swamp frogs
provide backup.

We are in no hurry
to go home.

William R. Stoddart
PITTSBURGH, PENNSYLVANIA

William is a poet and story writer. His fiction and poems have appeared in journals such as *The Pedestal Magazine, Adirondack Review, Ruminate Magazine*, and *The Molotov Cocktail*. Recent and forthcoming work is in *Third Wednesday, Maryland Literary Review, The Orchards Poetry Journal* and *Crack the Spine Literary Magazine*.
E: bill_stoddart@yahoo.com

OLD FRIEND

This to an old lost friend
who said long ago in the chill
of late October that she was leaving,
taking her mood of charcoal pictures.

I remember your face after
you told me to go away, the wind
changed it, carrying young words
to heaven. From the wings of eagles
you planned to sue God Almighty

to stop the voices. They made you
paint darkness – a brother dead
from the smash of physics
on a wrong-way road,
the nail marked hand

in the black confessional, the
way uncle looked at you when you
still trusted. That's when it stopped:
The conversations with adults, parents,
priests, nuns, friends. Our friendship

was a trap without bait,an itch
scratched until it bled raw tears
in the sharp October light.

Wanting me to remember the sky
that day, I saw furrowed clouds,
and how they made the foreshortened
illusion of infinity, like silvery chords
frozen in blue, fading slowly like vapour trails
through a fallow sky.

R. Bremner
GLEN RIDGE, NEW JERSEY

R. Bremner's careers have included stints as cab driver, security guard, truck unloader, and 38 years as computer programmer, including five years at Pan American World Airways. He writes of incense, peppermints, and the colour of time in such venues as *International Poetry Review, Anthem: a Leonard Cohen Tribute Anthology, Jerry Jazz Musician, Paterson Literary Review, Climate of Opinion: Sigmund Freud in Poetry, Poets Online*, and others. He appeared in the legendary first issue of the *Passaic Review* in 1979, an issue which also featured Allen Ginsberg. Ron has published seven books of poetry, including *Absurd* (Cajun Mutt Press) and *Hungry words* (Alien Buddha Press). He has thrice won Honourable Mention in the Allen Ginsberg awards, and has featured at the prestigious Bowery Poetry Club in New York's East Village, and at the ANT Bookstore, Montclair Library, Paterson Poetry Festival, Paterson Library, Gallery U, Brownstone Poets, Gainville Café, Creativity Caravan, and elsewhere. He lives with his beautiful sociologist wife, son, and dog Ariel.

E: rongnan3@gmail.com

MY BEST FRIEND AT 27 YEARS IN 1979

Billy Joe has positioned the piano carefully
in the corner where, if he squeezes past the pingpong table,
he can reach it, but playing is painful in these poor acoustics.

Pip's Lounge no longer keeps a piano, and so
Billy Joe prepares to enter a programming school
following in my profitable footsteps
as fulltime pragmatist and part-time poet.

He will play his beautiful melodies upon the 370/145
and, I still pray, before attentive crowds someday.

Rose Menyon Heflin
MADISON, WISCONSIN

Originally from southern Kentucky, Rose Menyon Heflin is an emerging poet and artist who loves travel and all aspects of the natural world. She majored in Environmental Studies and East Asian Languages and Cultures at Beloit College. Among other venues, her poetry has recently been published or is forthcoming in *50 Haikus, Ariel Chart, Asahi Haikuist Network, Bramble, The Closed Eye Open, The Daily Drunk, Deep South Magazine, Dreich Magazine, Eastern Structures, The Ekphrastic Review, Haikuniverse, Heartfelt Poetry Collection* (an anthology by Wingless Dreamer Publications), *The Light Ekphrastic, Littoral Magazine, Please See Me, Plum Tree Tavern, Poetry and Covid, Red Alder Review, Red Eft Review, Sparked Literary Magazine, The Texas Poetry Calendar, Three Line Poetry, Trouvaille Review, Visual Verse, The Wisconsin Poets' Calendar*, and *The Writers Club*. Her poetry recently won a Merit Award from Arts for All Wisconsin.
E: rosemenyonheflin@gmail.com

SON
For M.S.

My heart broke for you a little
That first time
I heard you call your little boy "son,"
Knowing it was probably
What you had longed to hear yourself
From the father who abandoned you
And wondering if it was what
The favourite uncle
Who took you under his wing
Used to call you.

As a woman,
I never really realized
How loaded that word could be,
But hearing you say it
As you patted your child on the head
And knowing your history,
I realized it was fraught
With a deep undercurrent of emotion,
Of masculine expectation,
Of pride and of need,
That I could never truly understand.

When I hear
The cherish in your voice,
I know the simple word
Holds profound masculine meaning,
Sure, maybe it's significance
Is all a social construct,
But you have bought into it,
Despite your pretend rebellion,
And it clearly carries
Great weight for you.

The defiance part of me
Wants to point out
That its built on manipulation,

That it sounds too old-fashioned
As a term of endearment,
But the part of me

That cares for my friend
And wants to see him happy
Silences her
And the voice that screams
Sexism at the lack of
A mother-daughter equivalent.

So, I let the word
And all its fake
Societal meanings and significance
Go uncharacteristically unexcoriated,
Focusing instead
On what it quietly but obviously
Means to you.

ON LOSS AND RECONNECTION: TWO TANKA

I.
Just the two of us
Wreaking havoc like old times
Chaos of friendship
Here today, gone tomorrow
Back again somehow at last

II.
Acutely felt loss
A dagger plunged in the heart
Bonded together
Reunion is a smooth balm
On wounds long turned gangrenous

Nancy Shiffrin
SANTA MONICA, CALIFORNIA

Nancy earned her BA at California State College, Northridge, her MA studying with Anais Nin. She earned her PhD at The Union Institute studying Jewish-American women authors. Her writing has appeared in the *Los Angeles Times, New York Quarterly, Earth's Daughters, Lummox Journal, The Canadian Jewish Outlook, A Cafe in Space, Religion and Literature, Shofar,* and numerous other publications. She has received awards and honourable mentions from The Academy of American Poets, The Poetry Society of America, The Alice Jackson Foundation, The Dora Teitelboim Foundation. Her currently available collection of poems is *The Vast Unknowing*, (Infinity Publishing, 2012). She resides in California with her husband the novelist Thomas Page.

E: nshiffrin@earthlink.net

W: www.NancyShiffrin.net

ONE LAST CONVERSATION
For Nan Hunt

are all our creations
stored in our ovaries awaiting fertilization
who would I bring back from the dead
should I have banged on your door
stood outside with a sign called the police
when you did not return my messages
last night I sat with poets
wondered why anyone would cry
to be in the *American Poetry Review*

a man read to his lover dead of AIDS
how he became acutely aware of
beeping sounds – I thought of us
meeting in coffee shops
me interviewing you for the *LA Times*
you wanted me to see
your laundry your laddered stockings
I never revealed how gut stabbed I felt
when I saw your letter of complaint.

I want to say I almost died
but had to come back and clean up
I want to say my family shuns me
I want to say meet me at
Coogies for iced tea and pie
except Coogies just closed
clowns impersonate me
fools write versions of my works
your voice is still inside me
pushing for strongest language

I don't think you'd like this chit-chat
it doesn't have dreams
I think you'd give me a hug
you'd be glad I got married
coach my astronaut-in-training
down from a sheer cliff
assure her brother he will find love
wherever you are you cheer me on
as I sing for the revolution
gather new friends
recite fresh poems

Rita B. Rose

LONG ISLAND, NEW YORK

Rita is an award-winning American poet, and her poems have been published internationally. Books include; *the chilling exposé, Asylum: from the inside*, *Veranda Sundown: twisted poetry and prose*, and her latest collection of pantoum poetry is *Flower Poems: Personalities in Bloom*.
E: Stonewallrusty@aol.com

I LOVE US NOW
For Con Artist

I. First Light Woodstock

Crescent lips; a fiery spark
unhurried, they reflect your soul
in my arms you nestle
quite content as we linger
imprints of our days ... our nights
indissoluble; the bond we share
desire lives in our heart; fluid is want
evocative are pledges whispered in the dawn
on loves mystic waves ...

II. Mid-afternoon Tea

Laughter and affection fit like a glove;
it is our life song — the you and me —
I never tire as I admire your dewy midnight face
your enchanting warm eyes and flaxen hair
early on in years I desired to take liberties
but dared not for fear of being dismissed;
of being left behind on this delightful path ...
And, enjoying our noon tisane, I have come
to learn your sips of adoration was equally so
it has been an unspoken commitment
on a vacillating, yet the fondest sea ...

III. Twilight Years

'I love us now' is our constant stake;
it is gentle ... superb ...
It is grander than to have lost to a one-time affair
throughout eternity we have remained devoted
nurtured is the embrace; our lover's ballet
you, with unending fondness
me, basking by your side
blessed are we to be
invited there
loving us now and forever
yonder the stars
beyond eternity
the sweet of heart we share...

Mariana Mcdonald
ATLANTA, GEORGIA

Mariana is a poet, writer, scientist, and activist. Her poetry has appeared in numerous publications, including *Crab Orchard Review, Lunch Ticket, The New Verse News, Les Femmes Folles, Southern Women's Review, We Are Antifa, Poetry in Flight/Poesía en Vuelo, The World Is Charged: Poetic Engagements with Gerard Manley Hopkins, Stone Sea and Sky, An Anthology of Georgia Poems, Fables of the Eco-future,* and *Anthology of Southern Poets: Georgia.* She co-authored with Margaret Randall *Dominga Rescues the Flag/Dominga rescata la bandera, the story of black Puerto Rican heroine Dominga de la Cruz.*

E: marianamcd@yahoo.com

APOLOGY

Ever friends, allow no doubt
this needs be the colour of our fate,
ours a vivid hue that shouts
as we the world variegate.

Among friends a query forms:
How much like a mirror might be
 - amid the placid and the storms -
I for you and you for me?

Being friends, is it unkind
to let the searching heart explore
a union of the soul and mind
touching to the spirit's core?

Often friends turn blinded eyes
from thoughts that can engender fears,
wondering if the jagged sighs
will make the friendship spill with tears.

Ever friends, no question mark
may join the grammar of our fate.
No need for dictums' inked bark:
love will our meaning punctuate.

PIECE OF SUN IN MY HEART

you are with me every day
piece of sun in my heart

you are with me in the car
piece of wind in my ears

you are with me on the path
piece of sky in my eyes

you are with me in the joy
piece of smile in my spirit

you are with me in the storm
piece of rain in my mind

you are with me in the night
piece of moon in my soul

you are with me in the dark
piece of fire in my breast

you are with me every day
piece of sun in my heart

Ermira Mitre Kokomani
CLIFTON, NEW JERSEY

Ermira is a bilingual poet, essayist and translator. She has published poetry, short stories and scientific papers in Albania and the US. Last year her book of poetry *The Soul's Gravity* was published in Albanian. Her poetry has appeared in *Jerry Jazz Musician,* (New York, 2020), *Sequoyah Cherokee River Journal 7*, (October, 2020), *Live Encounters*, (December, 2020), CAPS book *Mightier-Poets for Social Justice* (New York, 2020), and international anthologies *Musings during a Pandemic, I Can't Breathe* (Kistrech Poetry Festival, Kenya, 2020), *Rutherford Red Wheelbarrow 13*, (New Jersey, 2020), *A New World, Mediterranean Poetry 2019*, Montclair Write Group anthology, *NJ 2018*, Brownstone Poets anthology, and a range of other print and online publications. Ermira has also translated from Albanian into English the fiction novel *The King's Shadow,* authored by Viktor Canosinaj. She has majored in English Language, and has taught writing in NJ colleges for some years. She works for Rutgers University libraries, is a member of Montclair Writers' Group and Red Wheelbarrow Poet, and regularly reads her poetry in Open Mic events in New Jersey, New York, and France.
E: emitre1@yahoo.com

OUR HOLY CRAFT

O' friends,
I have sung this song for you,
and I sing it till today,
for very long has been our journey
travelling in our holy craft,
at those shores of sisterly love,
for days, and months, and years.

O' friends,
it matters little, so very little,
if birth brought us at a split second,
or under an equal Star,
for we are the shiny stars
who bonded with each other,
under the same space and time,
when we shook tightly our hands,
felt heart's glow heated our flesh,
as the Sun warms up the Earth.

O' friends
I have sung this song for so long,
and I sing it till today,
for sisterhood is a twin souls' conception,
where our hearts beat in a similar cage,
where double kisses on clock hands,
bear forgiveness beyond repentance.
For sonority, this innocent shelter
besieges us quietly with compassion,
dries out worries and dissolves our despair.
For fraternity this humane, willy face
yearns for us in sunny and rainy days,
as a mirror to strip naked our souls
to worship this temple cross-legged.

O' friends,
I have sung this song for so long,
and I sing it till today,
for you are the gentle morning dawn,
the silky violet that smooths souls,
perennial spring that knocks at the doors
of the clear, blue and endless dome,
where thoughts move and flow like clouds,

sometimes big, joyful and wise,
sometimes quieted, swollen and darkened.

O' friends,
The friendship's vessel is a hot oven
where our sincere love and faith melts
passing the shrinkage and swelling tests.
It is the souls' mechanism that
with fiery letters and shiny diamonds,
laces queen's wreaths for dear pals.
O' friends, hear my promise!
I continue to sing this song on friendship,
and I will sing it from my heart, always!

Judy DeCroce
NEW YORK STATE

Judy is a internationally published poet, flash fiction writer, educator, and avid reader, whose works have been published by *The BeZINE, Brown Bag Online, North of Oxford, The Poet Magazine, Amethyst Review, OPEN: Journal of Arts & Letters*, and many other journals and anthologies. And recently one of her poems was selected for a *Vita Brevis Press, Brought to Sight & Swept Away, A Poetry Anthology About Time* that went to number one in the New Poetry Anthologies category in Amazon. As a professional storyteller and teacher of that genre, she also offers, workshops for all ages in flash fiction. Judy lives and works in upstate New York with her husband poet/artist, Antoni Ooto.
E: judydecroce@yahoo.com
LinkedIn: @JudyDeCroce

HUEY AND ME AFTER THE GIG
Inspired by Hayden Carruth's love of Jazz

We was just talkin'...
not out the door

times going way back
comin' in

how it is—
sittin' and talkin'—

windas dark
diner bright—

rememerin'
all them clubs.

Look around
that us ...

Old?
Maybe that what you see.

Age drop off
when we jammin' late.

That's Huey an me—
we just talkin'...

not out the door.

Antoni Ooto
NEW YORK STATE

Antoni lives and works in upstate New York with his wife poet/storyteller, Judy DeCroce. Antoni is an internationally published poet and flash fiction writer, as well as being well-known for his abstract expressionist art. He now adds his voice to poetry; reading and studying the works of many poets has opened another means of self-expression. His recent poems have been published in *Amethyst Review, The BeZine, The Poet Magazine, The Active Muse, The Wild Word*, and a number of journals and anthologies.

E: antoniotoart@gmail.com
W: www.ooto.org
LinkedIn: @antoniooto

SCOUT

Do you still watch the door?

After all this emptier time
what should we make of our days together.

I don't know why it is
me staying, you going.

We had the same gate in our step,
mine, a chronic shamble,
yours, with a confident plumy tail.

And we teamed in the woods
where, around the burn barrel
you guarded with one eye open,
dozing, content.

Yes, content, both of us.

As seasons change, the days shorten.
Let this morning bring what it will.

I'm going for a walk now.
Your leash is still handy.

I get used to changes.

A BLESSING TO LEAVE WITH
For Jackie Trobia

Perhaps this is a trick;
another way of teasing me
when I think of you—
and I do so often,

I admire your tenacity
which keeps us together,
just a little longer.

On that rainy afternoon,
we came quickly,
because time was short.

Waiting … you remembered
something I needed to know.
Then nodding, searched for
a blessing to leave with.

       I offered a smile …
and you took it.

Previously published in the *Alchemy Spoon* Issue #3 Spring, 2021.

ELLEN
For Ellen

she had held things tightly
even friends, creasing memories

when she passed
all her fears of leaving left with her

only her rooms remained
different reflections of love

a favourite chair
           the coral Afghan
                   photos
                          music

and those air mails in a box
marked "SAVE"

Gary Shulman
PALM SPRINGS, CALIFORNIA

Gary Shulman, MS. Ed, spent a lifetime supporting vulnerable families and children. He began his career working with children with and without disabilities in an inclusive Head Start program in Brooklyn NY. He then transitioned to become the Special Needs and Early Childhood Coordinator for the Brooklyn Children's Museum for ten years. His passion for advocacy grew as he worked more and more with parents of children with disabilities. For over 24 years he passionately advocated for the needs of these parents as the Social Services and Training Director for Resources for Children with Special Needs, Inc. in NYC. The last eight years of his working life, Gary served as a private Special Needs Consultant, conducting hundreds of training sessions throughout NYC, and beyond, to help parents and professionals find and access the services and systems required to facilitate maximizing the potential of their children with disabilities. Now happily retired, he still volunteers his time any way he can to provide information to those in need of his expertise.
E: shulman.gary@yahoo.com
W: www.garyshulman.jimdo.com

TO A GOOD FRIEND WITH LOVE

With grace and power that only passion can create
She commands our attention and seals our fate
To always love her and share joy from her plate
A plate so generous it feeds us all
All who need a hand when we're about to fall
A teacher, a mentor, a mother a friend
A life-force so strong it cannot bend
Bend to the powers that try to hold her down
For love keeps her moving forward with hardly a frown
A small detour in the road of life
May cause our friend some temporary strife
But this we know and this we shall declare
That victory will be hers
And in that victory we will all gloriously share

SEASONS TRAVERSE OUR LIVES

Winter, Spring, Summer and Fall
The cycles traverse our days
If life has truly blessed you
Love comes in many ways
The smell of a balmy Spring flower
The majesty of winter snow on your tongue
A steamy refreshing summer shower
The falling of leaves and a sweet Autumn song
But no greater love can ever manifest
Than the comfortable enduring kind
Of a well seasoned lasting love story
That forever keeps you young in your mind

Nate McCall
SALEM, OREGON

What started as a way to express emotion, turned poetry into a burning passion Nate seeks to share with others. As an emerging poet, he uses a more formalized rhyming style for most of his writing, as he believes it allows for the most powerful expression of the whirlpool of emotions he has inside. He lives with his Alaskan Shepherd Malamute mix dog, who is one of the loves of his life and a continual source of energy and inspiration. He is currently in pursuit of a bachelors degree in English with a humanities concentration, as well as a minor in philosophy. These two subjects have pushed him to grow as an artist and think deeply about the world. He aspires to see his poetry impact people in a positive manner that helps them see light and life in a world filled with darkness. His inspiration for poetry comes from everything he sees and doesn't see around him, with the biggest source coming from his faith as a Christian.

E: nathanielmccall@corban.edu

ANOTHER SECOND OF ETERNITY

Is this what it's like?
To watch you walk away
My mouth is open wide
My heart wants you to stay

I know it's just a season
A second in the eclipse
Yet every second you were around
Life felt like a peaceful bliss

The last two minutes you were here
I barely got to say hi
Tell you about the stupidity of Dark
Then was forced to say goodbye

Could that eternity last a little longer?
The smile, those glasses, that hair.
I know it's foolish to write about this
But I still wish you were there

A fractured second, spun into hours
A minute as long as a day
That's the depth of the memory you left
And the depth of desire to see you stay

Just a little longer, a few seconds more
Traverse me to another of your worlds
Tell me about the fan-fiction you're reading
While the smoothie in the blender sputters and swirls

Hold back just another second of eternity
Goodbyes are hard to see
But this is honestly just the beginning
I'll see you in Fall, and continue this story

SEMESTER'S END

No goodbyes
The briefest of waves
The wind has picked up
Their voices lost in the caves

Gone to the wind
Forgotten to time
Some ill see soon
Some ill never find

Why does the beginning
Start at the end
Some wear caps and gowns
Perfectly fit and hemmed

Others just walk away
Packed bags leaving dorms
Knowing they'll come back soon
In large and loving swarms

But to those of us remaining
Their presence disappearing
Leaves an aching desire for time
Of voices, we were used to hearing

Now silence fills the void
A vacuum sucking out life
A playful malamutes growl
The only sound left wielding a knife

Can I even shed tears of loss?
I know most will return
But going back to a state of limited people
With endless time I seek to burn

Has it's limit with my energy
Even to an introvert like me
Because that tank will never get close
To being 2/3rds empty

I wish I could have had more time
But semesters come and go

Some of you I will see next year
Others will have to wait till there's snow

Nila Bartley
OHIO

Nila is recently married and lives in Ohio with her husband. She is middle-aged and enjoys being so. She has a new perspective that came with these new phases of life, which shows in her writing; her writing reflects her outlook. Nila wants to inspire people who read her work to contemplate the good things in life like love and laughter. This world can be a dark place at times and she likes to remind people of the better things, and derives a great deal of satisfaction from creating this; if she can brighten someone's day or week with what she has created in a poem or short story, she feels a sense of completeness. This feeling comes from using her God-given gift of writing for the betterment of a fellow human being. To take a person, even if it is only for a moment in time, to a place where he or she reflects on the good things in this life is a reward in and of itself to Nila.

FRIENDSHIP

Friendship is meeting your friend halfway up life's mountain
It is drinking together from life's fountain

The fountain from which love, compassion and commitment flow
True friendship must have these to continue to grow

Growing and maturing as we journey up life's mountain always
together come what may
Together the giants of life's mountain we slay

Climbing up life's mountain one may come upon rugged terrain
We need each other's help to endure - from separate journey's we
must refrain

Life's mountain can also have pitfalls and dangers
To these things my friend and I are not strangers

Of these things we have traversed together before
Because of my friend, fear grips me no more

Travelling life's mountain together - each other's problems we bear
Better together is how we fare

While scaling up life's mountain, decisions must be made and I hear
many voices
With my friend's help I make the right choices

Grappling up life's mountain side by side we go and reach the crest
I realize true friendship means always giving your best

Mark O. Decker
OCEAN VIEW, DELAWARE

Mark is a retired investment banker and businessman, and served in the White House during the administrations of Presidents Richard M. Nixon and Gerald R. Ford. He started writing poetry in 1968, and has been writing ever since. After retiring in 2016, he decided to organize his life's work of poetry in order to preserve it for his children and grandchildren. As a result, he started self-publishing his poetry, and has published several books of poetry since. At the same time he started sharing some of his poetry with his family and friends and, because of the positive reaction he received, as well as through various writer's groups he belongs to in Virginia and Delaware, he began submitting his words to both poetry journals and publishers. In 1972, Mark received a BA degree in education from Kent State University, and in 1977 he completed law school with a Juris Doctor degree from Antonio Scalila School of Law in Arlington, Virginia. He is happily married to Maureen McEwan, and they have three children - Mark, Jr., Susan and Kelly and (as of this moment), nine grandchildren.
E: mdeckersr@gmail.com

FRIENDS ARE FRIENDS ARE FRIENDS

This is unreal,
talking with friends,
true friends, old friends;
Being with people
that passed a big part
of their growing years together;
We all breathed fresh Woodsfield air,
goofed on each other,
Took math and spelling tests together,
Drank beer, and boogied;
Here we are reminiscing;
It's over,
three short days
of living, reliving and laughing,
loving a way of life
that seems so foreign to me now;
Friends are friends are friends;
I'll see you same time, next year;
Same way, next time.

FRIENDS

When your heart aches, and
The world is crashing all around you, and
pitiful, noiseless sound is emitted from your head;
Look around, you'll see your friends;
When you're down and being kicked,
poked and jabbed and pricked;
When tragedy and error
force you into their corner
with their wicked, wicked stick;
Just look around,
you'll notice who your friends are;
When you're sick at heart, and
aching for just one warm spot, and
everything you do seems to be for naught, and
you've made a fatal error
from which you're taught
many lessons that others have never sought;
Look around you, far and wide around you;
You will see your friends and foes,
and others;
Oh, those others.

END

POETRY WRITING COURSE

"Transforming your ideas into words, and your words into poetry."

Introduction

Aimed mainly at the new and emerging poet, and writers exploring poetry for the first time, packed full of tasks and research points, THE POET's new distance-learning *Poetry Writing Course* takes you through the elements that make amazing poetry, and the skills, methods and techniques you can use to begin exploring poetry for the first time, or to help develop and better your own work.

This Poetry Writing Course focuses on getting you, the student, to practise writing poetry across a wide range of styles, themes and topics.

The learning objectives of this course are:

- To give you a basic knowledge of the history of poetry.
- To recognise and be able to experiment with key poetic structures.
- To understand key poetic terms, techniques and devices, and how to apply them to your own poetry.
- To be able to write in a range of poetic forms.
- To recognise and develop your own style, and demonstrate your own poetic voice in your work.
- To be confident in your use of different poetic techniques such as rhyme, metre and figurative language.
- To be confident in experimenting with your poetry.
- To understand the importance of punctuation in meaning.
- To give you some tips and hints in approaching editors and submitting to publications.
- To understand the differences between finding a commercial publisher and self-publishing your own collection of poetry.

For further information go to:

www.THEPOETmagazine.org

and click on Poetry Writing Course

Compiled and published by:

Robin Barratt Publishing
Affordable Publishing Services

Books, Magazines, Newsletters, Websites.

www.RobinBarratt.co.uk

Printed in Great Britain
by Amazon

64144728R00129